opening our minds

avoiding abusive relationships
and authoritarian groups

jon atack

Trentvalley ltd., Colchester, England

Readers may contact the publisher at:
20 Meyrick Crescent, Colchester, CO2 7QY, UK

cover design by Spike Robinson

ISBN: 978-1-9196258-0-5

Fourth Edition
July 2021

this book is dedicated to the memory of Bobby Yang who was a daily
source of good cheer throughout his short life

Praise for this book:

"*Opening Our Minds* shines a laser beam into every key bit of research on manipulating the human mind and surgically extracts the kernel in each. This has created a book of immense breadth and depth without the lumbering weight of an academic tome. Instead, we have an almost breathless, short yet comprehensive review of what we know about manipulating human minds and the educational vaccinations against these processes. If there were a required reading list for maintaining one's critical thinking in the over-information age, *Opening Our Minds* would be at the top. Parents should make this book the first present to your children graduating middle-school, high school or college, and then bring it to your book club to discuss how to integrate it in your own life. It will be the liveliest discussion you have all year and very possibly the most worthwhile!"

~ **Ira Chaleff**, author *Courageous Followership,* and *Intelligent Disobedience.* Visiting Leadership Scholar, Moller Institute, Churchill College, Cambridge University. Chairman Emeritus of The Congressional Management Foundation, Washington, DC, and member of the Board of Directors of the International Leadership Association 2012 – 2017.

"Jon Atack's book *Opening Our Minds* is exactly what I expected: an interesting, important and incredibly helpful book. The work perfectly illustrates Jon's brilliance, learning, wisdom and compassion." ~ **James A. Beverley**, Research Professor, Tyndale University, Toronto, Ontario. Associate Director, Institute for the Study of American Religion, Woodway, Texas

"In the years I have sought to undo the abuses of extremist authoritarian sects and other controlling relationships, I have been one of many voices asking, "Isn't there anything we can do to prevent all this harm in the first place?" For a number of reasons, answering that question always proved harder than asking it. As more years have passed the techniques of propaganda, destructive manipulation, and predatory influence, once most often associated with totalist sects, now have penetrated into all areas of life.

"In this edition of his book *Opening Our Minds*, Jon Atack gives us clear insights and precision tools for protecting ourselves and our society from these exploitative techniques. He does this not merely by describing the current landscape of coercion, control, and harm, but by exposing the underlying principles by which our minds are vulnerable. In doing this, Jon also shows us how to equip ourselves to recognize and resist manipulation in all its disguises.

"This book has been on my "must-read" booklist for members, ex-members, and their families since it was first published under the title, *Opening Minds*. This new edition will remain there." ~ **Christian Szurko**, Dialog-Centre UK

"Opening Minds" by Jon Atack is an excellent guide for those people who want to understand what cultic mind control is, how it functions, and how not to become a victim of it. The book is clear, witty and deep at the same time. The author shows incredible erudition in many areas and possesses a rare gift of explaining difficult matters in a very simple and understandable way. I especially want to commend the language - concise and elegant. Bravo, Jon!" ~ **Professor Alexander Dvorkin**

"Jon Atack's book is an important wake-up call for us all. I work with people who have survived authoritarian groups and strongly recommend it to all survivors of human predators, and to their loved ones and the counselors who support them.

"Jon not only explains how human predators operate and why they are so successful, he also shows why we are all vulnerable to persuasion and trickery. It is important to know that acknowledging this makes us less vulnerable and increases our ability to help others who have been victimized.

"Jon is a truly gifted writer and has made this complex subject accessible to those who need it the most." - **Frances Peters**, counselor and cult expert.

"Jon has written a classic. He uses story-telling effectively to bring the book to life. *Opening Our Minds* orients the reader and provides an understandable framework for how our minds work, and how intelligent and functional people can become victims of undue influence.

"It will help you understand unethical influence in a wide variety of contexts including cults, parental alienation, terrorist recruitment, and more. Consider buying copies to donate to your local library, mental health professionals, politicians, and educators.

"Hopefully, this book will be translated in all languages and it will serve as a foundation to create global awareness about how humans can be deceived, manipulated, and enslaved so we can protect human rights everywhere." - **Steven Hassan**, PhD, director of Freedom of Mind and author of *Combating Cult Mind Control.*

Contents

before we begin

Human predators roam among us. Although there aren't many of them, they have a tremendous influence. To them, the rest of us are prey. Predators manipulate their prey using well-tried tricks. Once you know these tricks, it is much easier to avoid them or to stop them in their tracks.

Every bad relationship, every destructive group, every dangerous government has a human predator at its heart.

Predators rely upon persuasion. In honest persuasion, we have access to all of the facts – and different opinions about those facts – and enough time and privacy to consider these facts and opinions.

But then there is the type of persuasion used by predators, which is simply manipulation. To manipulate means to manage or influence skillfully, especially in an unfair manner.[1] Facts are hidden or distorted, and we are rushed into decisions that take away our own authority and harm our interests.

Predators cause upset, conflict, corruption and devastation. By seeing through their methods, we can take power away from human predators and have a much greater chance to overcome the problems they cause in our personal and group relationships.

Here is a quick description of the human predator:

Human predators:
- are mean.
- are utterly selfish.
- pretend friendship and love but feel absolutely nothing for others.
- are charming and good at flattery, but don't mean a single word of it.
- brag and boast and make up outrageous lies. When challenged, they blame others.
- don't feel anxiety or fear - or are deeply anxious and cowardly.
- are impulsive and easily bored. They demand thrills and take dangerous risks. They enjoy pushing others into taking dangerous risks, too.

- are bullies with explosive tempers.
- are cunning and manipulative.
- enjoy humiliating people.
- weaken people with insults and putdowns.
- hate it if anyone else has power or is praised. For the predator, life is a competition and they want to WIN.
- lie easily and think nothing of breaking a promise.
- are without conscience: they do not feel remorse or guilt.
- often boast about the harm they've done other people.
- are parasites and lazy, living off others, giving as little as possible in return.
- are control freaks, stopping others from taking control of anything if they can.
- force petty rules on others – rules that are impossible to follow.
- boast about tricking other people and breaking the law.

This book will show you how to deal with predators and how to make society safe from their tricks and traps.

introduction

The most precious and personal part of every person is his or her own mind. No one else ever sees it, or knows exactly what it is thinking or feeling. It is our most sacred possession because it houses our innermost identity. It defines for us precisely who we are, and who we are not. We can hide the truth from others, but not from ourselves. Or so we think.

But our mind, like our body, needs nourishment. Other people feed our mind with thoughts, suggestions, comments and ideas. We choose which ones to accept and which ones to reject. And we feel confident that we are good at doing so. But are we?

To be good at protecting our minds we must be familiar with the tactics and strategies that may be used by others to outmaneuver our natural protections and defenses. You can see a punch coming, but not a carefully crafted lie or manipulation strategy, unless you are trained to look.

The greatest threat to the autonomy of our mind is from people who seek to influence it for their own best interests, but present themselves as our friends and helpers. Every one of us has great confidence in our ability to protect ourselves from other people acting in ways that would harm our own best interests. We have faith that we have a strong mind, have good "crap detectors" and are not easily influenced. I call this "The Myth of the Unmalleable Mind." As kids are fond of saying, "Sticks and stones can break my bones, but words can never hurt me." But they can.

For the last 60 years I have studied how people can be fooled, seduced, altered and injured by con artists with exquisite expertise in mental manipulation. I have journeyed through Soviet, Chinese, Korean and American government programs to mentally enslave citizens and enemies, and private cultic groups around the world that have millions of devout followers. I have studied the tactics of advertisers and marketing specialists, the techniques of police interrogators, the dark literature of the antisocial uses of hypnosis, and the exquisite artistry of rhetoric and persuasion.

During this journey I encountered Jon Atack and found a fellow traveler, and a friend. My journey has been as a research scholar; Jon's journey began by being a victim. After he freed himself from the clutches of a cultic group, he chose to make saving others his life's work. There are very few "warriors of the mind." Jon is one of the best.

In this book, Jon has written a handbook for mental integrity. A botanist studies what insects and pests can harm plants and flowers. Jon has provided us with a handbook for protecting the mind from often invisible forces seeking surreptitiously to undermine freedom of thought.

One of the fastest growing areas of law is the expansion of protection for victims of mental assault. British and American law for over 500 years has recognized that it is a violation to act towards another person with undue influence. The cases, however, usually involved older people conned out of their life savings by dishonest caretakers. These cases involve *financial* harm. Within the last twenty years, however, courts and legislatures have recognized that undue influence can also include *mental* harm. New laws now widen the protections available for people injured by mind manipulators. The need for such laws demonstrates how serious the problem has become.

Lord Thomas Robert Dewar once observed that "minds are like parachutes; they only function when open." This book is a manual for keeping your mind open. If you want to make your body stronger, go to a gym. If you want to make your mind stronger, pay close attention to what this book tells you. Not only will you learn how to spot and avoid threats to your mental integrity, you will also have the pleasure of reading a very fine book.

~Alan Scheflin, professor emeritus of law

Alan Scheflin holds a BA in philosophy (with high honors), a JD in law (with honors), an LLM in law, and an MA in counseling psychology. He is the co-author of *The Mind Manipulators* (1978) and *Trance on Trial* (1989) and many others. He has also published over 70 articles, and is the recipient of 18 awards from various professional organizations including the American Psychiatric Association, the American Psychological Association, and the American Society of Clinical Hypnosis. He has been a consultant in, or appeared as an expert witness in, dozens of legal cases.

1
the web of influence

"When you believe in things that you don't understand, then you suffer." ~
Stevie Wonder, Superstition.

It doesn't matter how smart you are. Anyone can be taken in by a human
predator. Even an expert on influence.

you are not a gentleman

I was barely awake when the phone rang. The urgent voice at the other
end of the line claimed that Microsoft had found a serious problem with
my computer. The caller insisted that I log in, immediately: otherwise, the
malware would destroy my machine and everything on it. He sounded
deeply concerned.

I tapped in the letters as he dictated them. A list of over a thousand errors
and warnings scrolled down the screen. Yes, I had noticed that the computer
had been slowing down. Yes, so many error messages were indeed worrying.
"You see," he said, "your computer is about to die." I was having a little difficulty making out his accent; I was concentrating on understanding, rather
than on the significance of the call itself.

But I was beginning to wake up. "Did you say you're with Microsoft?"
I asked.

"No, we're partners. We're Microsoft certified. Look on your screen."

Sure enough, there was a window with "Microsoft Gold Certified" right
there, on the screen. Again, he insisted that my computer would die, *today*,
if I did not let him install software to quarantine the many infections. A new

window flashed on the screen. For £149 (about $200), he would save my computer, and the protection would last for a year, but for another hundred pounds, if I bought the software immediately – today – he would extend the protection to five years.

"How do I know that you're Microsoft certified?" I asked, stifling a yawn.

"Look at your screen," he responded.

"Yes, but you can put whatever you want on the screen. Who can I contact at Microsoft, in the UK?"

The address for Microsoft in London flashed on the screen. "But the London office won't know who we are," he said.

"How did you get my number?" I asked.

"If you don't do this right now, your computer will die. What difference does it make to me? I'm paid my salary whether you take my advice or not. I don't work for a commission. You'll lose everything on your computer. It's no skin off my nose."

"How did you get my number?" I asked again.

"You are not a gentleman!" he said. "I'm trying to help you." He sounded genuinely frustrated.

"Hang on a minute," I said. "I won't let you call me names just because I want to be sure your offer is genuine."

"It's no skin off my nose," he repeated.

"I want to talk to your supervisor," I said.

The supervisor came on the line and apologized for the slur. He then repeated the assertion that my computer would die, and I would lose everything on it, if I didn't act *immediately*. "Listen. We'll do the work for free. If you're happy, you can pay us. If not, you can simply walk away without paying a penny."

I put the phone down as my computer went through various changes before my eyes. I called my brother Jim. "Switch your machine off, immediately," he urged. "It's a scam. Several of my friends have been caught by it. They leave ransom-ware on the machine, so every few months, you have to buy new add-ons to repair it."

I had already pulled the plug. The phone rang again. It was the supervisor. "You've dropped your Internet connection. You are not a gentleman!"

"I *am* a gentleman and *you* are a scam artist. A criminal." He wanted to argue the point. I hung up.

Luckily, my son Ben is a computer expert and later that day he cleaned the machine thoroughly. "Watch out for any pop-ups," he recommended.

I have spent a lifetime studying tricks and scams. I can recite the litany of names used by experts to describe these manipulative methods. And yet, I almost fell for this rather obvious confidence trick. There are even web pages warning about this particular company.

I didn't buy the fake fix, and no ransomware was left in my computer. I've never sent money to a Nigerian offering to share his inheritance with me if I just give him a few dollars so he can collect. I have never sent a "registration fee" to collect my winnings from the Dutch lottery. When a gorgeous Malaysian girl claimed to lust after my aging body, I did realize it was a scam (though only after exchanging emails for a couple of hours).

It is not just the Internet that is rife with scams. Trickery is an aspect of human nature, and it reaches back long before the advent of the worldwide web. Indeed, some students of animal behavior say that lying is the first stage in the evolution of intelligence. Californian jays have been observed pretending to bury food, and then quickly concealing their actual stash, while their rivals scrabble about in the false hiding place.

Pride does indeed come before a fall. If there is one lesson that we should all learn, and relearn, as often as necessary, it is that no one is invulnerable to persuasion. Not even those of us who make it our life's work. Indeed, *it is confidence in our invulnerability that makes us so vulnerable.* Despite decades of immersion in the world of tricksters, I, too, can still be charmed, cajoled, and led like a lamb to the slaughter.

Years ago, I finished my interview with a teenager who had escaped from a notorious authoritarian group only weeks before. He grinned and said, "The great thing is, Jon, that we'll *never* be conned again."

I shook my head, "No, the great thing is that I realize I'm gullible. And that's my only defense. Whenever I'm brimming over with enthusiasm and ready to reach for my wallet, I try to stop myself and analyze the evidence. Sometimes that saves me money and embarrassment."

A few years ago, when Amazon contacted me to say I'd won a thousand pounds in their Wishlist lottery, I didn't believe it. And the disbelief did me no harm; it actually made it sweeter when the credit appeared in my account.

the fraudster's sales kit

The phone fraudster – and his colleagues in a boiler room somewhere in Kolkata or Delhi – went through a tried-and-tested script that exploited normal feelings and responses. First, he created fear: your machine will die.

Emotional pressure always reduces the capacity to reason. Language can be crafted to direct us away from thinking: psychologists have found that certain words and phrases can by-pass our reasoning processes altogether – "buy now", "new and improved", "for a limited time only" and "every penny counts", for instance.

Next, he created a sense of urgency: he wanted me to act immediately, so that I would have no time to think. This is the "buy now" mechanism, which slips past reasoning. When we are buying anything – from computer software or a second-hand car, to a business training program, to a new religion – it is important to take our time. This mechanism is recognized legally in some countries, where there is a "cooling off" period in which you can cancel a contract to fit double-glazing or anything else you have been pressured into buying. *If you must "buy now," don't buy at all.*

A good scam artist creates rapport. Here the phone scammer failed. He was too urgent, and he was rude. Often as not, when challenged, tricksters protest too much. How could I doubt his word? This is actually a way of generating rapport in reverse. He was suggesting that we had made a connection and that I had violated it by distrusting him. Whenever I hear the phrase: "You can trust me," a voice in my mind whispers: "You can trust me; I'm a con artist."

a fraudster's sales kit
- inertia – keep them going in the right direction
- emotional pressure – turn on the heat!
- urgency – don't give them time to think
- rapport – act like a friend and they'll trust you
- consistency – if you can get 'em once…
- flocking – "everybody's doing it!"
- scarcity – "supplies are limited!"
- reciprocity – "let me give you something in return"

Rapport is an essential aspect of sales and recruitment. We are far more likely to buy from someone who has become a friend. Instant friendship is almost always a trap. Real friendship takes more than one meeting, just as love at first sight is often simply a matter of psychological projection. We find what we are searching for in the other person, whether it is there or not, because *expectation conditions experience.*

From rapport comes *authority.* We believe our friends, but we also believe people who agree with us, and share our view of the world. Flattery usually works very well at creating rapport, and when someone has shown us that they have the discernment to appreciate our superior qualities, we are open to their opinions about other matters, too.

Once we have sent the first few dollars to the Nigerian heir, the Dutch lottery official or the gorgeous young Malaysian woman, the next tranche of cash comes more easily. Against the protests of her family, one seventy-year-old squandered her every last cent – some $300,000 – on a telephone scammer. She lost her home and ended her days on welfare, after alienating her whole family. The power of persuasion is far greater than we like to admit.[2]

Once we have committed to a course of action, we tend to continue. It is the inertia of "throwing good money after bad," which is also known as the *sunk cost fallacy.* Once we've decided on a course of action, we tend to keep following it down the slippery slope. Psychologist Robert Cialdini calls this *consistency* or *commitment.*[3] Scammers attack the most generous part of our nature. They are like vultures looking out for the kindest people. Somehow by continuing to fund the Nigerian's lifestyle, we believe that everything will work out. History is littered with such scams.

fraudsters in history

In the early eighteenth century, the Mississippi Company, owned by the French Royal Bank, offered investors the chance to make enormous rewards by buying shares in the new Louisiana Territories in America. The currency of France came to depend on the illusory trade of this company. Many French people lost everything they owned to the fraudulent Mississippi Company, and the French currency collapsed. At the same time, British investors were gulled into buying shares in the South Sea Bubble. The Panama Canal scam bankrupted investors in the Victorian era. Clever, wealthy and accomplished people lost everything.

Dishonest dealings also featured in the Wall Street Crash that precipitated the Great Depression in the 1930s. Share prices were inflated in an ever-increasing spiral. With the Crash, the banks, which had poured investors' money into this illusion, were forced to foreclose on mortgages; property prices collapsed. Later on, the same trickery happened on a grand scale with the banking crash of 2008. Bankers really believed that they could package up "sub-prime" debts and so give them value. So, property mortgages were offered to people who had no chance of making the payments.

The Headlong Fools Plunge into South Sea Water.
But the Sly Long-heads Wade with Caution ater.
The First are Drowning but the Wise Last
Venture no Deeper than the knees or Waist.

A contemporary illustration showing investors in the South Sea Bubble falling like over-ripe fruit into the sea

Two economists were awarded Nobel prizes for "proving" that the economy would never collapse again. Trillions of dollars leached out of the economy because of this fanciful belief. Once the mind is convinced, it continues in the same direction — *inertia*, the commitment of consistency, bedevils human belief.

This highlights another innate problem of such scams: if other people flock to invest, we will be tempted to follow suit. This pattern of jumping on the bandwagon is sometimes called *social proof* or *flocking*.

Any examination of history shows that people can be brought to believe almost anything. At the extreme, this *flocking* behavior led Germans and Austrians to vote away the right to vote and put all power in the hands of a skinny, average-height, dark-haired Austrian, who proclaimed the era of the muscled, tall, blond, Aryan superman. Fifty million people died in the aftermath of this group delusion. Hitler refused to end the war, costing another million lives, because he believed that his followers deserved to die, because they had failed him. There is no safety in numbers when it comes to belief, and joining the crowd quite often leads to catastrophe.

scarcity and reciprocity

Throughout history, *scarcity* is another often-used aspect of confidence trickery. This can be the insistence that we "buy now" (or the computer will die) or the precious rarity of a "limited edition" of 10,000 coins, postage stamps or porcelain mice.

We also tend to feel obliged to give something in return. Charities will send a free ballpoint pen, a couple of cardboard table coasters, or some nametags along with a request for donations. This is the *reciprocity principle*. The supervisor who almost managed to scam me said he would fix my computer for free, and I should only pay if I was satisfied. The truth is that many people will pay up, after this seemingly friendly gesture, which is simply another way of building rapport. Then your computer will crash, and you'll be forced to buy the "add-ons".

Now we turn to the methods used by scammers, recruiters, radicalizers and pick-up artists to slide past our defenses and sell us anything from a time-share to a belief system.

recommended reading:

Robert Cialdini, *Influence: The Psychology of Persuasion*
Pratkanis and Shadel, *Weapons of Fraud*

2

recruitment and seduction: the way to unhappiness

"The saddest thing about any man, is that he be ignorant, and the most exciting thing is that he knows." ~ King Alfred the Great

The process of coercive control follows a predictable series of steps. First comes *contact*. This will either happen in person or through advertising, which comes in many forms: flyers, posters, mailings, books, media ads and articles are all used by authoritarian groups to lure new recruits. Many groups use street recruiters, and most have their own publications; some, including Scientology, have hired professional advertising agencies to refine their approach.[4] Public relations experts speak of interruption as the first step. They make contact by distracting your attention.

The Moonies and, more recently, militant Salafi Islamists, approach college freshmen. Jehovah's Witnesses, Mormons and LaRouchies knock on doors. The LaRouchies – followers of the late trickster Lyndon LaRouche – also use obituary columns to target grieving widows and widowers. Pseudo-Buddhist groups, such as the New Kadampa Tradition, have latched on to the craze for Mindfulness and use this in their pitch.

Contrary to popular myth, authoritarian groups seek competent recruits. Anyone with significant physical or mental problems, including drug or alcohol addiction, will be weeded out at the outset. There may also be certain groups that are not targeted – Scientology, for instance, avoids gay people, journalists, psychologists, psychiatrists, therapists, disabled people and communists.

Authoritarian groups can and do recruit intelligent people. Many followers are idealists, convinced that they are working towards a better world. Studies show that authoritarian group members are often middle-class and fairly well-educated.[5] They have higher than average IQs and perfectly normal personality profiles. Authoritarian group members do not present with any more emotional or psychiatric problems than the normal population. The same is true of terrorists. Detailed surveys of several terrorist groups have shown that members show little difference from the general population for mental illness, except for their practice of the anti-social beliefs of the group.[6]

Once contact is made, *rapport* is developed. The recruiter looks for common ground, agreement on cultural, political or religious biases. In Scientology, this is called the "reality factor". The intention is to create a friendly atmosphere.

An Al-Qaeda manual cautions the recruiter, "Don't criticize the candidate's behavior. Thank him for any help, even if it is just a little. Caution: don't disregard his opinion or his manner of thinking, but let him express his opinion even if it opposes yours … Be close to him in order to get to know more about his character."[7]

Krishnas handed out joss sticks and then asked for a donation, which follows the *principle of reciprocity*. One of my friends startled a Krishna recruiter by refusing either to make a donation or to return the recording of Temple songs he had just been given. Most people simply reached into their pockets and overpaid for the few pennies' worth of "Spiritual Sky" joss sticks. This would often lead to a conversation, which is the agenda hidden behind the approach. This approach is like a fishing lure – a bright object to attract attention. Moonies sold candy and flowers on the street, at vastly exaggerated prices. Scientologists offer a "free" personality test. There is no such thing as a free lunch; there is also no such thing as a free personality test.

By answering the 200-question test, you volunteer private information, and grant authority to the tester. The test was the work of Ray Kemp, a merchant seaman with no training in psychological testing. It is called the "Oxford Capacity Analysis" to give it a ring of authority (Kemp had no affiliation with Oxford University).

Recruitment checklist
- contact
- reciprocity and rapport

- flattery
- test resistance to group
- push fear of worsening
- elicit confession to gain authority
  (recruit following directions from here down)
- show understanding and sympathy
- bring to a peak experience
- demand testimonials to reinforce consistency
- induce guilt, phobias, and disgust

The prospective recruit will be *flattered* – called "love bombing" by the Moonies. Your appearance, beliefs or talents will be praised to the skies. Rapport is built and a false friendship is created. Recruiters see nothing wrong in this trickery, because it is believed to be for the greater good and it raises their own status in the group. Moonies speak of "heavenly deception". For the recruiter, it is another statistic, which will lead to praise from the group, just like a salesperson selling another car. Recruits, however, feel as if they have made a new friend, someone who resonates with their existing beliefs. By the time they realize that the recruiter was simply agreeing to be agreeable – and make a sale – it may be too late to retreat.

the buy-in

Any *resistance* to the group is then tested, unless the group represents itself under a false name (the Moonies have dozens of front groups, and refrain from mentioning that they are a "religion" at first contact). Scientologists are taught to dismiss media reports by saying that the media is untrustworthy: "You can't believe anything you read in the papers". Not one person *ever* disagreed with me when I used this line – such is the level of public distrust of the media.

Once rapport has been established, the recruiter will seek out the most significant difficulty in the recruit's life. In Scientology, this is called the "ruin": "What is ruining your life?" If the preceding steps have been followed closely, *most* people will offer up even their most secret troubles. Unless they've been hurt before by exposing their secrets, most people welcome sympathy for their problems. It is surprising how willing people are to share their deepest longings with complete strangers, as if there is a need to confess; this confession deepens rapport.

Scientology recruiters then push the target into *"fear of worsening"*. The recruit is exploited to feel discouraged about the "ruin". "I'm sure you've tried everything, but nothing has worked." *Confession* of troubles usually shifts the recruiter into a position of superiority, of authority. The recruit will be willing to follow directions from this point, almost like Pavlov's dogs, which salivated when a bell was rung, because they had learned to associate the sound with the offer of food.

Next, the recruiter will use the information from this confession to demonstrate that the recruit desperately needs the group to achieve positive change; Scientology recruiters call this step *"bringing to understanding"*. Sales manuals suggest that a story be made up to show sympathy: "I know a guy who had exactly the same problem. He took a few of our courses and everything started to work out for him." The "understanding" is that the group can solve whatever problem is presented – whether it is romantic, financial, work-related or spiritual – anything and everything can be resolved by the offered course, counseling or study program, so the recruiter has no difficulty in inventing a supporting story: the ends justify the deceptive means.

Various tricks can be used to convince a new recruit. Indeed, the process of recruitment can begin by creating a euphoric or peak experience. Simply focusing attention can bring about a euphoric or high state.

This creates a state of awe, which is found in the love at first sight, or infatuation (also called limerence). Awe can bring about a belief in the authority of the person who introduces it.

There are five routes to awe: vastness, beauty, skill, celebrity, and inexplicable events. The view from a mountain ridge or a vast night sky, the beauty of a painting or landscape, the skill of a craftsman, the allure of a film star, or an event that baffles us can all cause an elevated state, in which we find it more difficult to reason, so are more easily influenced.

Tricksters often use inexplicable events to capture a recruit. The event is presented as a miracle or a transcendent state. The trickster then seems to have special knowledge and may be seen as an expert about everything.[8] They have achieved authority over the recruit which can extend to every aspect of their lives.

The first course, seminar, or workshop will continue the love-bombing, while often using a hypnotic technique to bring about a peak experience. Given a long enough duration, any form of repetition, mimicry or fixation can lead to a euphoric altered state. Chanting, drumming, group singing, visual fixation – as in meditation or mindfulness – repetition of a word or phrase ("mantra meditation"), repeated movements, such as rocking or "davening", shaking, or walking meditations, all lead to an altered state. It is easy to mistake the feeling of euphoria for psychological or spiritual progress. But just because we feel high doesn't mean that we've actually achieved beneficial change – as any cocaine addict can testify.

Most people in western society are unfamiliar with the effects of eastern meditation, so they are delighted and surprised by the sense of wellbeing that floods them. Almost every former member of an authoritarian group that I've talked with had an initial peak experience and spent the remainder of their time in the group trying – and failing – to repeat it. It is likely that the peak experience is simply a release of dopamine or serotonin. These neurochemicals are the "reward" system of the brain, and are released during sex and by alcohol and drug use. In a group setting, surrounded by approving people, carefully designed techniques can lead to a powerful high in the new recruit. Yuval Laor has defined the fervent attachment brought about by manipulating awe.[9]

Testimonials are demanded for *reinforcement*. In Scientology these are called "success stories". This reinforces *consistency*: the more publicly and loudly you commit to a technique or experience, the more difficult it will be to repudiate it later. People trying to stop smoking are advised to tell all of their friends that they have given up, because, under the consistency principle, it will make it harder to admit defeat and light another cigarette.

We all suffer from *confirmation* or *myside bias*, where we justify our actions and dismiss anything that disagrees with our beliefs. There is a quality of inertia to all human activity; we keep going in the direction we're travelling. Delivering a testimonial reinforces the sense of belonging and further confirms our bias.

Often, members will be encouraged to confess their former sinful lives in front of the group. By humbling themselves in this way, people give ever more power to the group. Members come to believe that everything good can be attributed to the group's practices, and everything bad is their own fault.

This brings us to *groupthink*, a normal aspect of human psychology. *Induction of guilt* is a part of this, but the group will also induce phobias and disgust towards out-groups and critics. *As Hitler said: create an enemy to bind a group together.*

Often, as we shall now see, we simply follow the herd because we want to belong.

recommended material:

Steven Hassan, *Combating Cult Mind Control*
Yuval Laor, *Belief and Fervor* on YouTube

3
belonging

"In charge of who is there in charge of me?" ~ Jon Anderson, Yes, *Close to the Edge*

There are two types of authoritarians: those who lead and those who follow. Followers believe blindly in the leader's right to command, and the leaders believe blindly in the same right. Authoritarian groups are exclusive: the group must come before everything else, so the member must identify fervently with the group and its ideas. There are many ways to forge and strengthen attachment to an authoritarian group or individual. In a live-in group, members are quickly drawn into 24/7 membership. Isolation from the outside world may be part of the strategy, but there will be enough activities to pack the day, and, usually, not enough sleep to ever properly wake up. There can be restrictions on diet – usually the cheapest food possible, so often a high-sugar, high-carbohydrate diet, which can add to the lightheadedness of sleep deprivation.

Group activities, including dancing, singing, or reciting dogma all add to a natural sense of cohesion. Everything that is different to the surrounding society – language, dress, diet, dogma – can add to the sense of exclusiveness and amplify alienation from that society. Add to this the promise that the secrets of the universe, eternal life, or liberation from tyranny are just a few steps away, and you have a potent mix.

Some groups differentiate between inner and outer members (called "staff" and "public" in Scientology). As a "public" Scientologist, I was subjected to none of the trauma and humiliation of daily life suffered by "staff", who kept their awful living conditions secret from the "public".

Staff members may survive on the bare minimum of sleep and nourish-ment while working impossible hours; "public" members are allowed to sleep and eat properly (even encouraged to do so in Scientology). The core inner members, on the other hand, while often living in drastically worse living conditions, are led to believe that they are superior not only to the world at large, but also to the "public" of the group. This elitism is a vital aspect of membership. In private, staff Scientologists will belittle the celebrities they so eagerly recruit. Out of their earshot, celebrities are dismissed as "dilet-tantes" – mere amateurs.

a brief history of submission

The word "mystery" originated in the ancient world, where followers went through a series of secret initiations, culminating in a pretend death and resurrection, which led them to fervently believe that they would sur-vive physical death. Initiates were called *mystes* and they existed at Eleusis in Greece almost 4,000 years ago.[10] These groups offered a sense of superiority to their members.

Groups that promise secret knowledge are broadly called "gnostic". At the beginning of the Christian era, the most popular gnostic or mystery cult was that of Mithras, a demi-god who offered resurrection and eternal life to his followers.[11]

Early Christian Gnostic sects developed around similar practices, and called themselves the "*electoi*" or "elect". Some were convinced that by going through the seven gates of the planetary bodies after death and reciting the right passwords, heaven would be theirs for the taking.[12] Modern practices that rely on a series of steps, grades or initiations – such as the Rosicrucians, Freemasons as well as Scientology and NXIVM – are "neo-gnostic".

People take pride in the trappings of office: the uniforms and badges, the medals and titles. We love to feel superior, and all too readily accept a place in a hierarchy of membership.

Mormons pledge complete allegiance to their group, through their "Temple Endowments." Freemasons and Rosicrucians function as secret societies, and often form networks in public office.

In the UK, there are many Freemasons in the police and the judiciary. They keep their membership secret and, in absolute contradiction of public policy, prefer their co-cultists over others. A voluntary register for public officials to declare membership of the Freemasons was boycotted by the UK police in 2001.[13] A friend of mine who had been a policeman for 17 years told me that he had always been passed over for promotion, because he refused to join the Freemasons.

Secret societies, "old boy networks" and other cultic forms are central rather than peripheral in our world. In 2002, a Metropolitan Police report cautioned that organized crime had infiltrated these very networks through the Freemasons.[14] In 2018, MP Sarah Wollaston renewed calls for a register, specifically for MPs and journalists who belong to Masonic lodges. Her plea failed.[15]

By the time I left Scientology, I was at the end of the 25th of the then 27 available levels. The deference of other members towards me was part and parcel of the experience. They believed that I could read minds, see into the future, and move independently of my body. It is shocking to discover the amount of damage concealed by the many people who completed these levels before leaving the group – because we were told that our "first duty" was to protect the reputation of Scientology.[16] Despite James Randi's offer of a million dollars for proof, no Scientologist ever demonstrated the supposed paranormal abilities we were promised we would attain.

Scientology calls those who give money "Patrons", and various titles are offered according to the amount "donated" – so, for instance, Patrons Meritorious have given $250,000. In return, their names are published in magazines and inscribed on plaques.

This sort of elitism encourages an "us versus them" mentality, as well as simple black-or-white thinking. The group is good and right; so, any critic is bad and wrong. Members of the group are the *elect*: they will become powerful and prosperous, irresistible to the opposite sex, achieve enlightenment or enter the kingdom of heaven – unless (and until) they realize that the emperor wears not a single stitch of clothing.

reinforcement

Membership must be reinforced, so that recruits feel they belong. Status is important, but there will also be a resolute conviction that the group is right and that doubt is wrong. The group's beliefs are touted as scientifically true and/or spiritually correct. This leads to the strange situation where believers will put aside their own values in favor of the group's dogma, which is the test of a true believer. Psychiatrist Robert Jay Lifton called this "ideology over experience" or "doctrine over person".[17] A famous heart surgeon in the notorious Japanese group Aum Shinrikyo murdered patients at the behest of his leader, in spite of the Hippocratic Oath's provision to do no harm.[18]

A fanatic will believe that the murder of innocents is vital to bring about the Caliphate or the End Days, perhaps putting aside years of benevolent behavior to follow this ruthless path. If the leader says that salt is sweet, the follower may well taste that sweetness, just as those hypnotized will cheerfully eat an onion as if it were an apple – or, as followers of Lesego Daniel testify, believe that gasoline tastes like pineapple juice.[19]

Years after leaving an authoritarian group, members often still cling to the teachings or the leader. They have learned to internally reinforce the state induced by their fervor. The contradictions in their beliefs can be startling.

Ma Anand Sheela spent 39 months in prison. In her autobiography, she says that all of her wrongdoing was at the behest of Rajneesh (aka Bhagwan or Osho the Buddha) and that she was scapegoated by him. She speaks at length about his vindictive, deceitful behavior, and says that he took a massive amount of diazepam or valium (some 240mg) along with two sessions a day – each two hours long – sniffing laughing gas (nitrous oxide), yet, in the same autobiography, she says, "He is my eternal lover" and "This love is still there. It is forever ... I am proud and grateful to be part of this plan. I will not exchange this love for anything in the world..."[20]

Reinforcement is also behavioral. Each group has its own variations. Habits of dress, of speech, responses and rituals are all readily adopted. Radical Islamists often adopt what they believe to be traditional dress, with men growing beards and women covering their hair, or even their faces. Scientologists make locked-on eye contact – which can keep them in an altered state of consciousness, while asserting predatory dominance.

There will be thought-stopping rituals – Krishnas chant the Hare Krishna mantra if they feel challenged. Slogans are implanted to keep thought at bay. Phobias are induced, so that opponents are viewed as if in the grip of Satan and unworthy of attention. Scientologists, followers of NXIVM and Jehovah's Witnesses are urged to cease any communication with critics – Suppressive Persons or agents of the devil – and such "shunning" is commonplace in authoritarian groups: indeed, it is a defining factor when assessing the danger of a group. Ostracism is a benchmark of authoritarianism.

hard selling

Once members have committed to a group, the honeymoon period is over, and ruthless techniques are often used to increase that commitment. Hard selling is used shamelessly in Scientology. Talking about the extremely expensive exorcisms that constitute the secret "upper levels" of Scientology, leader Ron Hubbard said, "Advanced Courses are the most valuable service on the planet. Life insurance, houses, cars, stocks, bonds, college savings, all are transitory and impermanent … Advanced Courses … last forever and give immortality. There is nothing to compare with Advanced Courses. They are infinitely valuable and transcend time itself."

It costs at least a quarter of a million dollars to complete Scientology's "Bridge to Total Freedom."

Hubbard aged beyond his 62 years, in hiding, 1973

In a dispatch called *What is Life Worth? - The Importance of Hard Sell*, Hubbard said, "HARD SELL is … a MUST in dissemination and selling of services and materials." He also said, "You tell him that he is going to sign up right now and he is going to take it right now … One does not describe something, one commands something. You will find that a lot of people are in a more or less hypnotic daze … and they respond to direct commands in literature and ads. Hard Sell means insistence that people buy." Further, "You have to be willing to invade privacy, very definitely … [recruits] don't have any rights!"

Scientology "registrars" – or salespeople – are trained using hard-sell expert Les Dane's book *Big League Sales Closing Techniques*. Sales interviews can last whole days. I'm happy to report that towards the end of my involvement with Scientology, I refused to accept a money-lender's check, even after a 13-hour sales interview. The demanded interest rate was 30%. Many others have not been so lucky, and have lost everything they owned, simply to pay for "advanced courses." Inheritances are quickly hoovered into the group's bank accounts. Former members can be saddled with debt for the rest of their lives.

Many words are used to describe authoritarian groups. In the last few decades an ancient Roman term has gained a new, negative meaning. Let's look at the word "cult".

recommended reading:

Jon Atack, *Let's Sell These People a Piece of Blue Sky*

4

cults in our midst

"Cults are far from marginal, and those who join them are no different from you and me." ~ Margaret Singer and Janja Lalich[21]

cults or authoritarian groups?

Many groups use questionable techniques to maintain the loyalty or devotion of their followers. The popular term for these groups is "cult". Science is impossible without precise definitions, so we must be careful about the words we use.

Many sociologists speak of "new religious movements", but this term is even less precise than "cult", as such groups often have no religious pretensions, nor are they all especially "new". "New" means since the millenarian movements of the 1800s, according to the Encyclopedia Britannica;[22] since 1830, if the Latter Day Saints (or "Mormons") are taken to be the first "NRM"[23], or mostly "since the 1950s" according to Professor Eileen Barker.[24] "New Religious Movement" could be replaced with the more precise "belief system".[25]

The Latin root word *cultus* means "worship", but, since at least 1711 "cult" has meant simply "Devotion to a particular person or thing".[26] The transformation into a negative or *snarl* word happened only a few decades ago, but has been vigorously adopted by both some academics and the media. The same transition is now happening to the word "sect", proposed as an alternative to "cult" by Professor Bryan Wilson, who favored the term "new religious movement".[27]

Academics rightly seek a neutral term, but this can obscure the simple reality that some groups and relationships are destructive both towards others *and* towards their own followers. The designation "new religious movement" has been stretched so far that the Manson Family and the Nazis could be added to the list. To avoid the pejorative meanings associated with the word "cult", we will generally use the term "authoritarian group." It should be noted that even a "new religious movement" can be authoritarian.

However, Robert Jay Lifton's negative definition of a "cult" fits our meaning for an authoritarian group. In 2019, the world-renowned psychiatrist, historian and thinker said:

"I have insisted upon retaining the word 'cult' for groups that meet three criteria; first, a shift in worship from broad spiritual ideas to the person of a charismatic guru; second the active pursuit of a thought reform-like process that frequently stresses some kind of merger with the guru; and third, extensive exploitation from above (by the guru and the leading disciples) whether economic, sexual, or psychological – of the idealism of ordinary followers from below."[28]

authoritarians in our midst

The techniques of the scammer have been elevated to new heights in those destructive, authoritarian or *totalist* groups commonly known as *cults*. The term "totalist" or "totalitarian" refers to dictatorial leadership which allows no disagreement and has "total authority". Our concern is for any authoritarian group or relationship, wherever it fits on the spectrum between autonomy and totalism.

There is no democracy in an authoritarian group. These groups have proliferated in our society. Experts list as many as three thousand dangerous authoritarian groups in the US alone. Some claim to be religious or philosophical, some are political or offer supposed therapy, others promise revelations leading to wealth or success in relationship, yet others promise eternal life. There are many more "family" groups that cluster around an abusive individual who has total authority. The smallest authoritarian group consists of a single follower in an intimate relationship with an authoritarian partner. The dynamics of manipulation or coercive control are broadly the same: all create authoritarian or even totalist relationships.

This definition of a totalist cult – which can be applied to any authoritarian group or relationship – was arrived at by a group of experts under the direction of Professor Louis Jolyon West, MD:

"A group or movement exhibiting a great or excessive devotion or dedication to some person, idea, or thing, and employing unethical, manipulative or coercive techniques of persuasion and control designed to advance the goals of the group's leaders, to the possible or actual detriment of members, their families or the community."[29]

There is a general belief that only weak people are taken in by these authoritarian groups, but this simply isn't true. Many authoritarian groups hunt down the smartest and most capable. According to research, most members are "fairly well educated" and come from "normal, functioning families."[30] It is not uncommon to find scientists, doctors and lawyers in an authoritarian group. *Susceptibility has little to do with intelligence or general education.*

Most people join a totalist or authoritarian group at a time of transition, such as after a bereavement or break-up, or a move to a new town or a new job. Students in their first year away from home are particularly susceptible, as they are also making the important transition from adolescence into adulthood, and are more prone to the enthusiasm of infatuation. When familiar habits and routines are disrupted, we become more open to new ways, and, when those ways come in a friendly, welcoming package, it is easy to accept them without sufficient reflection.

There is a very broad range of groups that create dependence among members. Some derive from traditional religions; others – such as the Teachers or the Sullivanians – are based on a pseudo-therapy. Some claim to be business trainers, like Landmark Forum (est) or Lifespring, but also tout "self-realization." These groups have long since penetrated everyday life: today, many major corporations use variations on the training methods of these authoritarian groups. These approaches may be called "team building" or "assessment", but, in reality, they derive from the control techniques used by authoritarian leaders, and are designed to override critical thinking.

In this century, the most notorious form of authoritarianism is the terrorist group, but the dynamics of authoritarian behavior are also found in gangs, pedophile rings, among human traffickers and even in some of our most beloved institutions.

The horrifying child abuse scandals that have recently rocked the UK show how authority and unethical influence have often been used to maintain criminal and immoral activities within organizations directed by both church and state. This is possible because the same dynamics apply to all human behavior, and, until we are familiar with those dynamics, we will continue to fall prey to them.

manipulative groups

Our concern is solely for *authoritarian* or *totalist* groups, which control most aspects of their members' lives. Authoritarian groups simply have too much influence – an *undue influence* – on members' material and psychological well-being. They override the autonomy of their members, along with their human rights.

There is a continuum from relatively benign groups to the most extreme; from groups which merely have an unhealthy control of members' decision making, to those which send their members out to kill or cause their members' deaths.

In Japan, Aum Shinrikyo stockpiled enough nerve gas to kill four million people. The notorious Manson Family in California committed a series of horrific murders. The Indian Thuggees also committed murder as an aspect of their religious belief, giving us the word "thug".

Extreme political groups are also authoritarian in nature. The Soviets and the Nazis systematically murdered millions of people out of doctrinal belief – the eradication of the Kulak farmers by Stalin, or of Jews, Romanies, Blacks, Communists and Jehovah's Witnesses by Hitler. Stalin and Hitler were "total authoritarians" or *totalists*. Any country

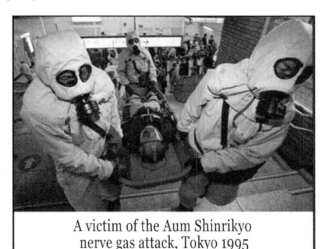

A victim of the Aum Shinrikyo
nerve gas attack, Tokyo 1995

that is ruled by a small, undemocratic élite is totalist.

Major religions have been guilty of profoundly anti-social behavior, such as the murder of tens of thousands by the European Christian churches during the centuries of witchcraft persecution. News continues to break about institutional child sexual abuse in mainstream Christian churches. The Watchtower Society of Jehovah's Witnesses, an international movement with perhaps eight million members, has refused to report thousands of its followers to civil authorities for such child abuse. In the High Court in England, in June 2015, the Watchtower Society was fined £275,000 for failing to protect a girl from abuse by a known predator, who was a Jehovah's Witness. In October 2018, it was ordered to pay $35 million by a Montana court.

These situations arise because authoritarian groups refuse their members' right to challenge fixed doctrines. *Wherever a group denies its members the right to challenge doctrine, it has moved onto the spectrum of manipulation.*

During the Middle Ages, two popes ordered excommunication – exclusion from heaven and eternal damnation – for any man who wore long hair.[31] We believe ourselves more enlightened, but bizarre doctrines continue to be enforced by many groups in our "free" society, for instance, the savage beatings and "paddling" of children in certain fundamentalist Christian groups in the US, which would be illegal in most of the western world.

A group of just two people can have the dynamics of an authoritarian group, if one rigidly determines the behavior of the other; or, as with the Jehovah's Witnesses, the group may number many millions. There are many variations of authoritarian relationship where decision-making is restricted to an authoritarian group or individual. This group or individual assumes the right to interpret – and even overlook – the rules. And they may be able to ignore even the plainest evidence that contradicts their belief system.

Authoritarian groups deny the right to freedom of opinion. Anyone who continues to doubt will be ostracized – turned away by family and friends who remain committed believers. Believers are told that defectors are ignorant, at best, or evil, at worst, and must be excluded, for the continued health and safety of the group.

There is nothing new here: traditionally, religions often exclude "heretics". The very word *heresy*, in its origin, means "choice" and applies to those who have chosen to disagree on some point of dogma. The word was long ago extended to mean *immorality* and even *sodomy*. With the advance of human rights, no mainstream religion would remove the right to doubt or question, as authoritarian groups do.

Some argue that even science is a belief system, and it is true that scientists have often refused to believe evidence, instead favoring the dogma of a fading paradigm; this does make their behavior cultic. It is also true that cliques of scientists have acted as authoritarian groups. For instance, under Trofim Lysenko, the Soviet Institute for Genetics outlawed any disagreement with his absurd ideas. Crops bred by the Institute failed and led to mass famine in both the Soviet Union and China.[32]

True science encourages disagreement and challenge, where authoritarian groups forbid either. This means that the word "scientist" does not signify any belief system, but membership in a community that constantly tests the truth of ideas about reality. Through the scientific method, hypotheses can be tested, based on observation and experiment, rather than belief. Science is a method, an approach to evidence, not a belief system.

With science, an idea or hypothesis is tested through an experiment that can both verify or falsify that hypothesis. Once an experiment has been independently replicated, the hypothesis becomes a theory. Science is based upon theories that offer the most likely explanation, and that can be challenged through new experiments, rather than a series of dogmatic declarations about the nature of humanity and the universe that are handed down without confirming evidence. *Only if a precept or principle makes sense and can be tested should it be adopted.*[33]

This leads us to a discussion of the deliberate use of manipulation and the difference between "brainwashing" and other forms of coercive control.

recommended reading:

Jon Atack, *Scientology: The Cult of Greed*
Ben Goldacre, *Bad Science*

5
manufacturing fanatics[34]

"[Socialist] militants accepted that feeling stressed, feeling conflicted, feeling confused were indications not that something was wrong but that something was right" ~ Janja Lalich, *Bounded Choice*[35]

Critics of the existence of coercive control often call it "brainwashing". As we shall see, the brutal "brainwashing" methods used in the Chinese "re-education" camps are far harsher than most approaches to coercive control. The word "brainwashing" is so emotionally loaded that it can halt debate, so it should be carefully defined, before we go any further.

brainwashing

When Mao gained control of China in October 1949, he instituted his cherished plan to enforce ideological conformity on every man, woman, and child across that vast terrain. He wanted to root out capitalist ideas in a single generation.

The Chinese phrase *hsi nao* – a pun on an ancient term referring to the cleansing of the heart and mind – gave the world the word "brainwashing". The term was first used in English in January 1950, in The Times of India, under the heading "Brain-Washing" where it was reported, "This is what Chinese papers graphically term 'washing one's brains,' or 'laying one's heart on the table.'"[36] The term was subsequently popularized by journalist Edward Hunter.

Chinese communists had been trained in Russia since the 1920s. The principal method was one of intense self-criticism or "thought struggle".

The thought reform program was described in the official publication *China Today,* in 1950: "The government has adopted the principle of making the greatest possible use of students, government personnel and other intellectuals of the old society. But the minds of such people are thickly encrusted with the ideology of the feudal gentry and the bourgeoisie. And while these people retain the viewpoint of the former ruling classes, they cannot carry out the program of the new government, which is based on the interests of the laboring class."[37]

The term "brainwashing" was the popular term for the official term "thought reform" or "ideological remolding" (*sixiang gaizao*),[38] which was developed by Mao's crony Liu Shou-ch'i from Stalin's thought reform program.[39]

Mao had put 200,000 0f his followers through the original program before he declared the conquest of mainland China complete.[40] Camps were then set up for the millions of dissenters.

Conditions were harsh, but not all prisoners were physically tortured or starved. Far more subtle means were used to break the will and bring about compliance (in China, millions have been subjected to this systematic program for years on end.[41] They claimed to have finally closed the camps at the end of 2019[42], but, at the time of writing, outside observers have not been allowed to check this claim).

Psychiatrist Robert Jay Lifton interviewed 40 returnees from the original camps over a period of 17 months. All had signed confessions to immoral acts that conflicted with their own beliefs and were either severe exaggerations or plainly untrue. After escaping from China, these thought reform subjects were baffled by their own admissions. Most accepted that they had believed these absurd declarations at the time of signing, but did not understand *how* they had come to believe them.

Lifton delineated eight aspects of the Chinese thought reform or coercive control program (which we will consider in detail). *Neither violence, nor even the threat of violence*, had been needed to achieve extreme shifts of belief. Among the victims were Catholic priests, who had confessed their part in an entirely fictitious political spy network directed by the Vatican. On their release, they were overwhelmed by guilt as their former beliefs flooded back.

China exported thought reform techniques, along with other more tangible weapons, to communist North Korea, where they were applied to devastating effect on the United Nations' POWs during the Korean War, from 1950 to 1953. The North Koreans paraded UN POWs who made untrue, and at times bizarre, accusations against their own armed forces and western democracy.[43] On their release, the POWs were mystified by their own statements.

There is strong evidence of a direct link between North Korean techniques and the world of cults through the Unification Church, or Moonies. Sun Myung Moon learned the techniques of thought reform as a victim, during three years' imprisonment in North Korea.

Moon created The International Federation for Victory Over Communism (VOC) in 1968. He ran this organization in parallel with his already established Unification Church. VOC was closely associated with the South Korean Central Intelligence Agency (KCIA)'s political "re-education" of communists. Former officers of the KCIA soon transferred their skills to the Moonies. The most significant convert was Bo Hi Pak, a colonel in the South Korean CIA before becoming Moon's right-hand man.[44]

Like Lifton, Berkeley psychology professor Margaret Singer studied subjects of "brainwashing" – returning POWs from Korea, and over the decades counseled some three thousand members of many types of authoritarian groups. She adopted the term "exploitative persuasion" to describe the insidious process of manipulation. Early on, Singer noted the similarities between POWs and those trapped in an authoritarian marriage – she pointed out that both are hostages, deprived of autonomous decision-making.

peer group pressure and the BITE model

Authoritarian groups control the behavior, information, thoughts and emotions of their members. Every society is a complex cultural web made up of commonly held beliefs, attitudes and behaviors. Only when displaced into an unfamiliar society do we fully realize the distinctive qualities of our own. Dropped into an alien culture – such as an authoritarian group – it is surprising how quickly people adapt. Most people will slide into the beliefs of a new group with little questioning.

We are susceptible to obedience because of our childhood training. We are also prone to agree with any group we belong to; a natural expression of groupthink. Authoritarian leaders rely upon both obedience and groupthink.

Authoritarianism represents a foreign social environment or *milieu*, where beliefs, attitudes and practices are different from the surrounding society. Robert Jay Lifton explains: "Through this milieu control the totalist environment seeks to establish domain over not only the individual's communication with the outside (all that he sees and hears, reads and writes, experiences, and expresses), but also – in its penetration of his inner life – over what we may speak of as his communication with himself."[45]

Psychologist Leon Festinger identified control of behavior, thought and emotion as salient aspects of transformation. Author, activist, and former member of the Moonies Steven Hassan added *information* to Leon Festinger's original model, so creating the behavior, information, thought and emotion – or BITE – model.[46]

Behavior Control
Information Control
Thought Control
Emotional Control

Changes in behavior, information sources, the channeling of thought, and the control of emotion are the path from one social group to another. Authority and respect that was given before to family, peers, or the larger society and its establishments, is transferred to the new group. The seed of fanaticism has been sown, and a new identity is being parasitically transplanted onto the existing self.

the tragedy of Omar

Margaret Singer added her own insights to those of Lifton's thought-reform model. To illustrate the full effect of coercive control, we will look at a specific example of extreme indoctrination, through the lens of Singer's model. While this young man's story ended in a dramatically unusual way, the stages of his radicalization followed an all-too-recognizable path.

Omar Khan Sharif was born in the heart of England, in Derby. Twenty-seven years later, his lifeless body washed up on a Tel Aviv beach, soon after his explosive belt had failed to detonate outside an Israeli nightclub.[47]

Omar Khan Sharif's father was an immigrant who had built a highly successful business through unremitting hard work. Omar was the youngest of six children, and his father had fond hopes that his son would become a doctor. To this end, Omar was sent to Foremarke Hall, which prepares boys for Repton, a prestigious and expensive private school. After three years, Omar dropped out, going on to complete his secondary education at a local state school instead.

Like many recruits of authoritarian groups, Omar was intelligent, socially accepted and fairly well-adjusted. Paul Elliot, a friend at Foremarke Hall, remarked that Omar "was such a nice, jovial guy at school. He fitted in well and was a really friendly person ... My fondest memory of him is that he used to have a Rubik magic trick – a flat thing with circles on it. He managed to break it during a religious instruction lesson. Everyone was laughing at him. He was definitely the class joker. We used to hang out as kids, doing everyday things like skateboarding. He was a great fan of football and we played together in the park at break time."[48]

During his teens, Omar's parents separated. Omar and his five siblings all took their mother's side. The separation did nothing to deter Omar from successfully completing his secondary education, and he was accepted as an undergraduate student in mathematics by King's College, in London. As a child, he had little interest in religion, but at King's he was approached by a recruiter for the UK chapter of the Islamist group Hizb-ut-Tahrir (which was soon afterwards banned from campus).

The recruiter used a well-rehearsed approach. He promised Omar a return to purity – forgiveness for whatever misdeeds now bothered him, and a life in paradise. The offerings of true faith were used as bait, and once the bait had been swallowed, and the hook taken, Omar soon became a true believer.

Omar was not to know that he had been systematically recruited. An

Al-Qaeda manual gives a checklist that demands the recruiter's responses after each meeting:

1. Is he eager to see you?
2. Does he talk with you about his private affairs and his hobbies?
3. Does he ask you to help fulfill his needs after Allah?
4. Does he follow your orders?
5. Has he told you that he loves you (for Allah)?
6. Has your fondness for him increased?
7. Does he love to spend a lot of time with you?
8. Does he accept your advice and respect your opinion?

If the score is: Less than 10 (*sic*), you didn't succeed, so choose another candidate and start from the beginning.

creating a new identity

Joining a new belief system often leads to significant changes in both behavior and appearance. Omar Khan Sharif had joined a new "in-group", and put a barrier between himself and the world, and his former life in that world. Once he had converted, Omar adopted old-fashioned clothes which set him apart. He put aside the normal social life of a young man at university, no longer visiting bars or going clubbing, and spent so much time studying his newfound belief that his degree work suffered badly. The changes in Omar's appearance and bearing were commented upon by those who knew him back at home.

In an attempt to make up for lost time in lectures, Omar borrowed notes from a female student. From this encounter, a romance blossomed, and she followed him into the group. By this time, Omar's father had died. During his second year, against his mother's wishes, Omar married the fellow student. Then he dropped out of university.

Omar's wife finished her degree. She realized that Omar was so obsessed by his activism that she would have to support them both. She took a job as a schoolteacher and, over the next few years, managed to combine breadwinning with giving birth to their three children. The marriage was rocky. Omar took the family abroad, intending to stay away for a year, but soon cut the trip short. His second trip was taken alone. Soon afterwards, his wife read that his lifeless body had been washed up on a foreign beach. Their youngest child was barely two months old.

Omar's immersion into an authoritarian group follows a sadly typical path. Omar Khan Sharif failed in a suicide bomb attack sponsored by Hamas in Tel Aviv, in April 2003. His companion, Asif Hanif, blew himself up and killed four people at Mike's Place, a popular bar.

Asif Hanif's friends in England were incredulous. At first, they thought that his identity must have been stolen. They could not believe that "Teddy Bear" Hanif, a bright and considerate student with a passion for cricket, could have been involved in a suicide attack. He had even spoken out against suicide attacks as a violation of the Qur'an.

The leader of Hizb-ut-Tahrir, Omar Bakri, was eventually expelled from Britain, but not long afterwards another member of the Hizb, Dr. Bilal Abdulla, was charged as the prime suspect in the car-bombing of Glasgow Airport.[49] He is now serving a life sentence.

The steps of Omar Khan Sharif's induction reveal the path followed by many recruits of a range of authoritarian groups. As psychologists Philip Zimbardo and Michael Lieppe said, "…indoctrination into terrorist groups often resembles the Moonie system."[50] This is relevant to all patterns of persuasion where the individual's choice is over-ridden, but, as we shall see later, it is also relevant to those who willingly choose to join a destructive organization.

Hanif and Sharif from their "martyr" video

accepting authoritarian beliefs

The first step of any authoritarian journey is dislocation, through either physical or psychological disorientation. In one or more ways, the recruit is dislocated, whether from the surrounding culture, or from a familiar way of life. Most often, the recruit is at a point of transition – in an unfamiliar place or at a turning point – and feels disorientated and unsure. New routines form when old ones perish. In a changed social environment, we are more malleable. It is easier to change old habits in new surroundings, whether those habits are good or bad.

Omar Kahn Sharif was the child of Kashmiri immigrants. Derby has a large Muslim Asian population, but they are displaced into a very different culture from their homeland. Omar's father was penniless when he arrived in England in 1962. Starting from scratch, he created a business empire that included fast food restaurants, a laundromat (or launderette), a health club, and an amusement arcade. But his enterprise left him little time for family life or for the niceties of his religion. Although Omar's father made sizeable contributions to the establishment of a mosque, a fellow student said that when Omar arrived at university, he knew little more about Islam than the formula of prayer.

The children of immigrants who have a different religious culture to that of the host country suffer a particular disorientation with regard to beliefs. Most will integrate into the host culture, reconciling the differences. However, a study of 165 Al-Qaeda members has shown that 129 of them – some 78% – were either the children of immigrants or were living away from their country of birth when recruited.[51]

In his important book, *The Islamist*, Ed Husain explains that most of the Muslim students at his college in London, "had no real bond with mainstream Britain," even when they had been born and raised in Britain, like Husain himself.[52] Ed Husain attended state schools and his devout, moderate Muslim family celebrated Christmas and regularly bought cakes from the local Jewish baker.[53]

College campuses have long been recruiting grounds for authoritarian groups. This is recognized by universities, which ban many such groups, including Hizb ut-Tahrir, the radical Islamist group that recruited Sharif. Hizb ut-Tahrir also picked off members of existing Muslim groups within universities. Ed Husain ran the radical Young Muslim Organization at his college when he was recruited by the Hizb.[54] Authoritarian groups are especially successful with new students, who have been dislocated from their homes, families and friends and are busy trying to create a new adult identity.

That said, dislocation – or transition – can happen at any time of life. Some groups scour the obituary columns to prey on the recently bereaved. The normal routines of a widow or widower have been irrevocably changed. *We are most vulnerable at turning points:* a new job, a new environment, or a lost relationship, for example. This means that the usual transition points of life create susceptibility, so adolescents and the elderly are generally more vulnerable.

In some instances, an entire society is dislocated by catastrophe, whether natural or man-made. This is true with nationalist or separatist groups. In this case, the key is the stability of the society. Poverty, plague and conflict have a dislocating effect.

deception and the hidden agenda

Authoritarian groups usually disguise their true intentions behind well-rehearsed claims. The Moonies have recruited on campus under a variety of names, including the Collegiate Association for Research into Principle. Recruits were not usually told that CARP was part of the Unification Church until they arrived at a Moonie camp. Moon's view that Christ was a failure and that he himself was the true Messiah would be kept back until enough enthusiasm had been generated by a carefully tailored program of indoctrination, love-bombing and sheer exhaustion.

Like the Moonies, Hizb has a roster of alternative names; once one is banned on campus, they can simply shift to another. This makes it practically impossible to ban such groups: like the Hydra, they just sprout new heads.[55]

At first approach, some Islamist groups claim to be charities that support orphanages, schools and hospitals. A senior Hamas official has candidly admitted that charitable activities are used to swell good feeling, so that Hamas can gain new recruits and greater political sway.[56] Hamas claimed both Omar Khan Sharif and his partner, Asif Hanif, as martyrs to their cause.

Sincere religious groups have an open agenda. If you want to become a monk or a nun, vows of poverty, chastity, and obedience will be explained in advance. The hardships of the life will also be explained, and the life itself will be experienced as a novice before vows are taken. An authoritarian group does not make the outcome of membership clear. Omar Khan Sharif was not approached with an offer to strap explosives to his body, so that he could blow himself and a group of innocents to kingdom come. *Deception is fundamental to exploitative persuasion.*

Omar Khan Sharif changed his behavior by adopting traditional Muslim garb and growing his beard. His wife covered her hair with the hijab. When challenged about these changes by old friends, Omar just smiled, refusing to enter into dialogue. Omar soon accepted the Hizb as the primary source of information and the arbiter of other sources of information. So, the *Qur'an* and the *Hadith*, the sayings of the Prophet, became central to his new understanding of the world. But Omar accepted the interpretation given to the *Qur'an* and the *Hadith* by the leaders of Hizb ut-Tahrir. Of course, these people are a minority: very few Islamic scholars interpret their scripture to encourage anti-social behavior in host countries, or to alienate Muslims from non-believers.[57]

When Omar Bakri Muhammad, the head of Hizb in Britain, fell out with its leaders in Lebanon, he funneled members into his own group, the now notorious al-Muhajiroun. This means "the emigrants", a direct expression of their sense of dislocation, which is particularly telling, because many of its members were, like Omar Khan Sharif and Ed Husain, not emigrants at all, but British citizens, born and bred. Omar Khan Sharif's time was so bound up in the group that he stopped attending university lectures. For the first time in his life, he performed *namaz* – the five times daily prayer. This normal Muslim practice was an aspect of his new life for Omar, not simply an expression of faith.

Group members are urged to follow the behavior of the group, often by changing their style of dress, their habits of speech and their demeanor. They ignore or ridicule sources of information that disagree with the group.

Groups often take complete control of a member's time, but they can also lead the member to set aside certain times each day to attend classes or meetings, or to read or distribute literature, meditate or pray. Those members who do not enter the group's environment may set up a private shrine at home or put a picture of their leader in a prominent place. A new environment or *milieu* is created.

Thoughts and emotions are brought into line with the doctrine taught by the leaders. Over time, guilt is instilled for thoughts or feelings in contradiction with the teaching and impossible standards are imposed: for example, a young man who feels desire for a woman is considered sinful – even more so if he feels desire for another man (Daesh/ISIS have murdered many homosexuals). Positive feelings for non-believers, even parents, siblings or children, are immoral. Behavior, information, thoughts and emotions come under the control of the group.

While in the Young Muslim Organization (YMO), Ed Husain was expected to ask permission before attending other groups' meetings.[58] In accord with the Al-Qaeda recruiting manual, members filled out a "routine sheet" each day, including the number of new recruits they had "targeted" and had to report their contributions to YMO every week. Husain says, "those who underperformed were often subjected to strict questioning."[59] Interrogation is a common aspect of authoritarian behavior.

authority – the leader as infallible guru

In an authoritarian group, gang or abusive relationship, the guru, leader or dominant partner is seen as the ultimate *authority,* the fount of knowledge on all matters. Of course, such complete expertise is not possible.

We all have to rely on the knowledge and skill of experts, who have authority because of their experience with a subject. Such *expert authorities* exist in all walks of life, from surgeons, doctors, and lawyers, to plumbers, mechanics, and electricians. We are often expected to accept the *rank authority* of those who are put in power above us, whether they have the necessary knowledge and skills or not. The guru extends this rank authority to all subjects and often pretends to be all-knowing.

It is sensible to question authority, until we understand what is being suggested, especially when our future depends upon it. However, in an authoritarian group, the leader, or leaders, become the sole authority on *everything*, regardless of qualification or experience. And the right to question is highly restricted.

This authority can reach down to the most trivial detail: Scientology's creator, Ron Hubbard, even gave mandatory instructions on how to clean windows – using old newspapers – or even on how to put flowers into a vase. Members can be reduced to infantile dependence: Hubbard went so far as to explain that it is important not to knock the vase against the tap or faucet.[60]

Submission to teachers is a tradition the world over. Obedience to the teacher is often absolute, and the literature of eastern and western cultures alike is filled with tales of disciples who have given up the right to make even simple decisions. In the East, to this day, apprentices in crafts and arts commonly submit to this sort of discipline. In spiritual pursuits, the *guru* becomes a father figure, a representative of God on earth. Indeed, authoritarian leader Osho (formerly Rajneesh) simply called himself "Bhagwan", which can mean either God or Buddha. Maharaji Prem Rawat is called "Lord of the Universe" by his devotees. With our modern liberal attitudes, we are aghast at the subservience offered to gurus, but such subservience is commonplace in authoritarian relationships. By forcing subservience on women, traditional religionists perpetuate authoritarianism in the form of gender apartheid.

"Bhagwan" Sri Rajneesh

Omar Khan Sharif came to view Omar Bakri as his guru, and his final actions accord with the path laid out by Bakri in his public statements. Ed Husain describes him as a canny speaker, saying, "there was not a non-Arab Muslim in the land who could argue with the wit and articulacy of Omar Bakri."[61]

Dependence on the authority figure by the follower is at the heart of manipulation. Although a competent and compassionate guru may help a pupil, the atmosphere of complete obedience and avoidance of questioning means that they can also pass on their shortcomings as if they were virtues. As authoritarian groups grow, so the contact with the guru reduces until there is little or no contact at all save from a small number of members. The guru is usually shielded from prolonged contact with all but this small group, so charisma is projected, with the guru becoming an idealized representation. This is important, as they rarely, if ever, live up to the idealized expectations they have created in their followers. As a group grows, it is the doctrine – the rulebook – which becomes the center of belief.

loaded language

Restrictions of language easily lead to restrictions of thought and feeling. Most of our thinking is mixed up in words. Language is associated with the emotions it evokes, so that "snarl" words and "purr" words cause automatic responses. Politicians refer to "fascism" and "appeasement" to create a subconscious link between their opponents and the dictatorships of the 1930s.[62] This method of associating ideas can be surprisingly effective. Slogans can circumvent analysis and fuel desire, as advertisers well know. *On the lips of the manipulator, language stifles thought, rather than encouraging it.*

Loaded language excludes outsiders, building a wall between the elitist in-crowd and the rest of the world. It is a private vocabulary with terms that are often difficult to translate, because they are fashioned from the group's own eccentric concepts. Having insisted that it is *essential* to understand every word exactly, Scientology has two dictionaries, each more than 500-pages long, so followers can decipher a phrase such as: "Don't get reasonable with dev-T caused by downtone downstats, SPs and degraded beings." Impenetrable jargon inevitably raises a barrier, but it gives the insider a sense of superiority, of special knowledge.

Unlike the technical language of the sciences, loaded language confuses rather than clarifies. Even simple ideas are twisted and packed with esoteric overtones. Words can even come to signify the opposite of their common meaning, rendering group conversations impenetrable to outsiders. To Scientologists, the word "reasonable" in the sentence above means giving in to other people's reasoning. So, unlike the rest of us, Scientologists work hard to be "unreasonable".

Omar Khan Sharif was introduced not only to the traditional religious language of Islam —necessary to understand the concepts of the faith – but also to new and loaded interpretations of traditional terms. So, he came to believe that he could become a *shahid*, a martyr for Islam, although the *Qur'an* clearly prohibits both suicide and the killing of innocents.[63] Omar wanted to become a holy warrior, a *mujahid*. He even spent three weeks training in Afghanistan. Non-believers were dismissed as *kaffirs*.

To Islamists, the term *jihad* has come to mean a war on non-Muslims and Muslims of other sects alike, rather than the struggle against tyranny and oppression.[64] Omar had entered a new world sharply bounded by what Lifton called "thought terminating clichés".[65]

Language is not confined to words: symbols can also be loaded. The swastika, already an ancient symbol of creation and illumination when the Buddhists ad-

Swastika on a statue of Buddha

opted it, was given a new and devastating meaning by the Nazis.[66] Symbols alone can trigger intense emotions, and emotions always cloud thought; the authoritarian leader wants to create a physical and psychological environment that keeps the emotions constantly aroused and reasoning subdued.

Gestures, when added to symbols and language, continue to reinforce membership of an exclusive group. Even the rituals of prayer can be perverted from their original meaning and used to arouse enmity towards *kaffirs*. Ed Husain speaks of the mechanical exactness with which members of one Islamist group pray.[67] Members may also recognize their fellows through secret signs and symbols, which bolster their sense of uniqueness.

An over-emphasis upon the meaning of words can hide the preposterous nature of a group's concepts. The recruit must absorb a large vocabulary, rather than carefully examining the concepts that underlie the words. Followers substitute pure unadulterated belief for understanding. If challenged, they insist that the leader's text is logical, although they cannot explain it. *Confusion is the gateway to suggestibility*, which can lead to submission to the authority of the creator of confusion.

the sense of powerlessness

Throughout the recruiting process, the individual's sense of *powerlessness* is emphasized. Personal problems, such as depression, ill health or familial conflict, are played upon.

The hidden fears of the recruit are exposed and the foundation for dependency laid, because the group offers to resolve those fears, whether in this life or a promised afterlife, or as a utopia – a heaven on earth – for future generations. *Idealism becomes a vulnerability, as idealistic people are eager to join a group that demands change, because they feel powerless to change a corrupt world on their own.*

Omar Khan Sharif was told about the international Islamic community, or *ummah*, and the urgent need to protect this community from the depredations of the West. He was told about the Caliphate that once administered the religious life of Islam.[68]

As an isolated individual, Omar was shown that he was completely powerless against the wealth and power of the West, and could do little to hinder the leaders of Islamic countries, who are reviled by Islamists. Then he was offered membership of a group that promised the triumph of the faith.

By adopting the views of the authoritarian group, Omar pushed his existing views into the background. He saw those views as part of the "brainwashing" accepted by the broader society. This aspect of information control robbed him of any external comparison for his new-found views. Any news item that disagreed with the group's propaganda was rejected as biased, or even rigged. Dissent was constantly undermined. Free discussion was discouraged, or even prohibited. Rival ideas were dismissed out of hand, and critics were smeared without any consideration of their criticism. This strengthened and rigidified the normal tendency to seek confirmation for beliefs and reject conflicting evidence.

Omar saw that all of his past attempts at resolving difficulties had failed, at this point, he had been opened up for indoctrination into the authoritarian group. In this final aspect of the control of the social environment, the peer group, the beliefs of the group have pierced the recruit's emotional core, so that behavior changes to fit in with the group's demands. There is no need for rational persuasion to play any part in this process. When completely surrounded by group members, very few people have the power to resist. In an authoritarian marriage, the dominant partner decides what will be believed.

the demand for purity

The group comes to represent the only island of purity in a world seen as toxic, treacherous and deceitful. Omar Bakri's followers lived by a strict code that put aside traditional Muslim practice in favor of radical political action. Bakri preached violent action and the overthrow of western governments. Although tolerated in Britain, Hizb ut-Tahrir was banned throughout the Middle East. Omar Bakri, the "Tottenham Ayatollah", had taken political asylum in Britain, and lived on state handouts for years, but he openly promoted the murder of the

Omar Bakri Muhammed

British Prime Minister to advance his own cause.

Essential to any guilt-manipulating code is this *demand for purity*. Developing guilt is essential so that members long to renounce every aspect of their former life. This is a key part of authoritarian conditioning, because it is here that a new identity is created, separating the person from the old values. Complex issues are reduced by simplistic polarization; everything is either black or white. There is no place for shades of grey in an absolutist scheme.

The teachings of the group are always right, and opponents are always wrong. Authoritarian groups insist that if you are not with them, you are against them. There is no middle ground, nor any time for consideration. Not only are there no innocents, there are *only* combatants. Omar Bakri taught that Israeli children were "legitimate targets", because, "if children are killed, the fault lies with the adult occupiers who brought them into a battlefield situation." According to Bakri, all of Israel is a "battlefield situation".[69]

Hizb and other Islamist groups use the traditional terms *haram* – forbidden – and *halal* – permitted – to shape unthinking polarization among followers. A welter of loaded language is added, often in Arabic, and usually redefined, so that the recruits – whose first language was usually either English or Urdu – would believe that they were being taught a coherent and long-established system of beliefs. In fact, the ideas of the Hizb stemmed from its founder, Taqiuddin al-Nabhani, who published his first book in 1950, and radically redefined traditional Islam, perverting it into a political philosophy.

Omar Khan Sharif felt ashamed of his life before the group. He had done a great deal that was *haram*. He had offended God by drinking alcohol, looking at pornography and indulging in the decadent lifestyle of contemporary British society. He longed to repent and make penance for his former sinful life.

Omar could not spare time to make a living and support his children, because he had to devote himself to purging his old, sinful self, while learning to avoid the temptations of the debauched world around him. Otherwise, he had no hope of eternal paradise.

Like any Muslim, Omar longed to know the *Qur'an* in its original Arabic: indeed, he wished to commit the whole text to memory. His teachers focused on conflict, violence and hatred in their interpretation. The world was not split into Muslim and non-Muslim, but Muslim and anti-Muslim. Where the Prophet Muhammad had accepted the other "religions of the book" – Judaism and Christianity – and gifted Islam a centuries-old tradition of tolerance towards these other beliefs, Omar was led to believe that Jews and Christians are locked in a crusade to destroy Islam. Omar was taught that any non-Muslim, whether man, woman or child, is a soldier of Iblis, the devil, so a legitimate target for *jihad* or holy war. Fellow Muslims who failed to accept the teaching of Nabhani were "partial Muslims" or "barking dogs".[70]

Normal urges toward pleasure can become a daily reminder of impurity and weakness. Purity easily becomes puritanical, with recruits even feeling guilt about their own health, happiness or good fortune, when compared to the misery of others.

Omar Khan Sharif became obsessed with the belief that he could only truly purify himself through martyrdom, to wash away all of his sins, and the endless stream of sinful thoughts became inevitable in such a controlling and guilt-ridden environment. As Lifton observes, "by defining and manipulating the criteria of purity, and then by conducting an all-out war upon impurity, the ideological totalists create a narrow world of guilt and shame. This is perpetuated by an ethos of continuous reform, a demand that one strive permanently and painfully for something which not only does not exist but is in fact alien to the human condition."[71]

Purity is accompanied by the insistence that the past is not only renounced, but painfully exposed to the light through confession. The recruit is kept in a state of remorse and vulnerability by reminders of past failure. The old personality is cast as the devil's dupe, a constant threat, able to regain power through a moment's lack of vigilance. Through confession, the recruit is kept in a constant state of humiliation and submission. And every day brings new temptations, dark urges, and impure thoughts to the guilt obsessed.

Of course, such guilt manipulation is a sour aspect of many relationships, where one partner constantly reminds the other of past failings. As with all manipulation, it leeches authority away from the individual, who loses self-trust and self-esteem, so becoming ever more dependent on the manipulator.

The recruit must believe that new attitudes, behavior and emotions have arisen spontaneously. Techniques which alter normal behavior – such as chanting, fasting, staring and other forms of perceptual fixation – may be used to induce euphoria, which is attributed to mystical insight.[72]

Those new to meditation are usually surprised by its results, and tend to attribute their experience to the guru, rather than seeing it as the normal physiological response to stillness and perceptual fixation (the Ganzfeld effect). There are many paths to euphoria, most of them perfectly acceptable in the proper setting. Traditional Muslim practice includes meditative prayer, repetition of the names of God, sleepless vigils and fasting. These methods can calm anxieties and heighten concentration, so relieving the tensions and pressures of the outside world, but they can also make a susceptible follower ever more prone to direction. Students of the *Qur'an* are encouraged to memorize the entire text by chanting out loud while rocking back and forth, rhythmically. This method of committing information to memory is highly effective, but it relies upon creating an altered state, which can easily be abused.

Omar Khan Sharif was no doubt grateful to Omar Bakri for offering resolution to the turmoil that raged inside him. He received this teaching as a special, personal gift, without realizing that it is the normal practice of most Islamic believers. Egged on by Bakri's enthusiastic support for the 9/11 bombers, and his gleeful predictions of home-grown terrorism, Omar Khan Sharif was inspired to follow the terrible path of the suicide bomber.

mystical manipulation

Expectation conditions experience, so in an authoritarian group, potential "realizations" are suggested before a technique is practiced. The recruit will be surprised by a "spontaneous" understanding that is exactly as predicted in the revelations of the leader's teaching. Sometimes, this extends to conjuring tricks that are claimed as miracles. Kneeling before Indian guru Sathya Sai Baba, devotees would feel a surge of energy, which they believed emanated from the master. In fact, the kneeler before his throne was electrically charged, so the surge of energy was simply an electrical current, but a miraculous interpretation was so strongly suggested that devotees never thought to question it. It took a skeptical Japanese TV crew to make the

Sai Baba

discovery. True believers dismissed the filmed footage, because the evidence of the senses is denied in authoritarian situations.

Victims of such planned "spontaneous" euphoric experiences believe that they have been initiated into a mystery and joined an élite. They are among the élite few who have understood the doctrine – whether it be Maoism, Nazism, or the views of an exclusive religion, therapy group, or sales organization. There is a mystical dimension, because the doctrine supported by these experiences is beyond rational understanding and so available only to the initiated.

Typically, these experiences lead to a feeling of oneness with the group and its leader and separation from the rest of humanity. The recruits are now among the chosen few, the illuminated, possessed of a special and unique understanding that is beyond the grasp of less developed or "evolved" people. The normal feeling of belonging to a family has been hijacked. The group is now the family, and this new family is, in turn, the greater self, to be supported at all costs, even unto death.

As Yuval Laor has pointed out, fervent believers will protect the authoritarian relationship as they would their own child. They become highly emotionally charged if any criticism is made of the group, the doctrine or the leader.

The recruit must come to exclude all doubts as sheer selfishness, and give absolute trust to the authority of the group and its leader. There is a "higher purpose" than the demands of everyday life, whether it be devotion to God or party, leader or nation. By this time, recruits will often sacrifice their own well-being, and that of anyone else, for the good of the cause. Decency and morality are bound up entirely in the teachings of the authoritarian group.

Normal values can completely reverse: for instance, followers of the Japanese authoritarian cult Aum Shinrikyo believed that through murder they were releasing victims from karmic debt, so speeding them to happier incarnations. With this absolute perversion of compassion at the center of their doctrine, Aum Shinrikyo had stockpiled chemicals to produce enough nerve gas to kill four million people. They believed fervently that an earthly paradise would come to exist through the annihilation of some peoples and the enslavement of others.[73]

the mystical imperative

Omar Khan Sharif took solace in the promise of a literal paradise. He was a highly intelligent young man, with a scientific education, completely alienated from the society around him. His only pleasure came in the thought of sacrifice to God. He had learned to surrender himself to the euphoria that came when he practiced the ritual prayer or read the *Qur'an*. The rest of life was a chore, something to be endured on the way to paradise. *This sense that real life is in the future is common to authoritarian groups: members live not for today, but for tomorrow.*

The recruit is manipulated into believing that there is a *mystical impera-tive* in the authoritarian group's doctrines, and that magical results will be obtained through absolute devotion to that imperative; that direction or command. The imperative is expressed through the will of the leader, so it must be followed absolutely, as if it were a precise formula.

Followers experience heightened states, which are perpetually rekindled through the symbols and the language of the group. They may come to believe that they will achieve supernatural powers, or that their group will overcome insuperable obstacles, by following the leader's order to the letter. When they fail, they will believe they did not follow some detail, or blame their own lack of purity, rather than the inadequacy of the order.

Militant Islamists have come to believe that, by attacking the West, they will precipitate a full-scale Muslim war against the non-Muslim com-munity, when, in reality, all that has been achieved is a more divisive and dangerous world. Omar Khan Sharif believed that by killing tourists, as well as the brave ambulance staff trying to help the victims of Hanif's bomb, he would contribute to the overthrow of Israel and the western democracies. Thankfully, his bomb failed, and he had no effect whatsoever, except to leave behind three fatherless children and a grieving widow.

Inside the group, recruits long to join the ranks of veteran members, so they imitate their behavior. Veterans, in turn, learn how to publicly pretend a superior state of being. The eager young Omar Khan Sharif wanted to be like the veterans of al-Muhajiroun. Eventually, he felt he had surpassed even the group's leader, and set out to join the activists. Omar Bakri talked about martyrdom to overthrow the unbelievers. Omar Khan Sharif decided that talk was not enough. He fulfilled his teacher's imperative and became a martyr – a *shahid*.

Both the committed authoritarian group member and the terrorist come to accept that the leader's insight is deeper than their own, and that the im-perative of the leader must be followed without question. The ideology of the authoritarian group sweeps away the existing experience of the recruit.

Where experience contradicts the view of the guru, that experience must be mistaken. Ed Husain challenged the poor religious practice of many members of the Hizb, and was surprised when Omar Bakri simply expressed agreement, but made no move to teach the proper formula of prayer, or encourage Arabic studies, in order to gain a better understanding of the *Qur'an*.[74]

ideology over experience – doctrine over person

Through the imperative of *ideology over experience*, the recruit sheds attitudes and beliefs achieved through direct personal experience, and even rigorous professional training, in exchange for the attitudes and beliefs of the thought-reforming manipulator. Contradictions dwell side by side, apparently unnoticed, in the recruit's mind. When interviewed, a former US Marine said a trainee, who had *threatened* to strike a Drill Instructor, was forced to stand through the night holding a 70-pound kitbag above his head. Whenever he fell, he was beaten with swagger sticks, until he resumed his stance. Yet, in the same interview, the former Marine claimed that he never saw any "unnecessary brutality" in the Marines. For him, there was no contradiction in these statements. He had been taught that there was no brutality, and he believed this sufficiently strongly to discount his own experience to the contrary.[75]

As Lifton said, "Rather than modify the myth in accordance with experience, the will to orthodoxy requires instead that men be modified in order to reaffirm the myth."[76] So, Omar Khan Sharif set about recasting his relatively normal English childhood as degenerate, and his family and friends as deluded sinners bound for hell. He listened as Omar Bakri gave his one-sided history of the enemies of Islam. He came to see any act of charity by a *kaffir* as a diabolic lure designed to sway him from his path.

Lifton explained that totalists demand that "character and identity be reshaped, not in accordance with one's special nature or potentialities, but rather to fit the rigid contours of the doctrinal mold."[77] This *doctrine over person* can lead to the rewriting of personal history to underplay, or even exclude, memories of dissonant experiences or reasoning. Often this consists of simply emphasizing or ignoring certain aspects of life before the group, but some groups employ supposed therapy systems that review the individual's past, and steadily construct false memories that reinforce the group's doctrine. Groups that believe in reincarnation can easily displace or reconstruct believers' memories. Believers can imagine links in former lives with the leader, and "remember" lives that are consistent with the mystical imperative of the group.

Followers come to believe the new life histories – the confessions – they have helped to construct. One former member of an authoritarian group told Margaret Singer that he had been a "drug addict" prior to his recruitment. Close questioning revealed that he had accepted this group interpretation of his pre-group drug experience: three tokes from a marijuana spliff.[78]

Any evidence which conflicts with the belief system is rejected without inspection. In dismissing any criticism, the recruit's rationalization will be as fabulous as it needs to be in order to justify the leader. The scientific application of Occam's razor is of no interest to the authoritarian believer: the simple explanation is by no means the most likely.[79] No matter how far-fetched and labyrinthine the leader's ideas are, they are true, because they stem from a deeper perception of reality. Where the accumulated weight of scientific evidence disagrees with the leader, then, as far as the follower is concerned, the scientists are plainly wrong.

Omar Khan Sharif came to see himself as a sinner who would only be forgiven and allowed the key to paradise through radical action. He became a terrorist, because he was absolutely convinced that it was the only way to save his soul.

These processes transform the individual into a follower, but to create a case-hardened True Believer, the new beliefs must be tempered to make them impervious to change. Otherwise, whenever followers leave the environment controlled by the group, they may float back into their former identity, just as all but one of the escapees from Chinese thought reform camps did in Lifton's groundbreaking study. The follower carries the group everywhere, just as a tortoise carries its shell. And just like a tortoise, the follower will retreat into that shell when attacked.

sacred science

Whether the authoritarian group is religious in nature or not, it becomes *sacred* to the follower. The leader is seen as an exemplary, archetypal hero who has overcome immense challenges, and exhibited astounding courage and insight to develop the teaching. Neither the teaching nor the teacher can be questioned, precisely because they are sacred. Through the *sacred science* of the teachings, the world shall be reformed.

Paradoxically, the teachings are also claimed to be rationally and scientifically valid. In Lifton's words, "Thus the ultimate moral vision becomes an ultimate science; and the man who dares to criticize it, or to harbor even unspoken alternative ideas, becomes not only immoral and irreverent, but also 'unscientific.'"[80] To the follower, the will of the leader is the measure of rationality. Anything that disagrees with it is irrational, preposterous, even.

Authoritarian leaders associate themselves with accepted authorities, and often claim academic qualifications that they do not actually possess. Such figures also assume titles to promote their importance. The second president of the Jehovah's Witnesses Watchtower Society adopted the title "Judge" Rutherford, to elevate himself. The Indian guru Rajneesh, called himself *Bhagwan*, or God or Buddha (believers now call him Osho the Buddha). Sun Myung Moon is called True Father by his followers. The founder of Transcendental Meditation is usually known by the title he immodestly bestowed upon himself: *Maharishi* or "great teacher." Maharaji has an even more bloated self-promotion: he is the *greatest* living teacher. Ron Hubbard was

"Judge" Rutherford

the "boss", the "Commodore", the "Old Man", the "Founder" and the "Source". He also claimed false academic credentials, including a university degree and a doctorate.[81]

If the rationality of a supposedly scientific doctrine is questioned, then it may be quickly relabeled a *sacred* doctrine, understood only by the leader, so beyond dispute.

Sacred science not only pretends scientific thinking, it often employs supposedly scientific apparatus. A long-term Scientologist told me that he had laughed out loud when he first read the group's secret OT 3 materials. But the group's lie detector – or E-meter – confirmed their accuracy for him.

He had never questioned the lie detector itself. He simply believed it to be a scientific instrument.

Many groups make exaggerated claims for their practices. Followers of Transcendental Meditation were told that they had brought down the Berlin Wall through meditation. The Kabbalah Center claims that the Zohar saved the lives of Jews who studied it under Nazi occupation (suggesting that the millions who died were "impure"). Such claims give an aura of miraculous, scientific power to the techniques, devices and texts of the group. Of course, *that which cannot be tested cannot by definition be considered scientific,* but this does nothing to stem the claims.

Members of the Hizb put aside centuries of scholarly interpretation of the *Qur'an,* instead adopting the sacred science put forward by Omar Bakri. All other realities must be shaped to the received word of God, as interpreted by their own leadership. This means that the subtlety of the text is easily lost, especially where it refers to customs that existed only at the time it was written, which may be easily displaced into modern times; for example, the necessity of military resistance which refers specifically to the defense of Muslims against attack, after the flight from Mecca to Medina. Islamists associate all outsiders with those Meccans who tried to kill the Prophet. Everyone who does not believe exactly what they believe – including fellow Muslims – is seen as an enemy trying to destroy them. In this way, paranoia replaces reason.

The various militant Islamist groups are also at war with one another. So, Hizb members revile Al-Qaeda, even though both are aberrant sects of the Sunni aspect of Islam. *To see the Hizb as representing conventional Muslim belief is akin to seeing the members of David Koresh's Branch Davidians at Waco representing all Christians.*

dispensing of existence – the route to genocide

The final and most terrible part of involvement in an authoritarian group is the sense of superiority that leads to individuation from the rest of humanity. Once such a belief is accepted, members see themselves as an élite, and cease to be concerned for the welfare of outsiders. At worst, only members of the group have the right to live. Opponents and even uncommitted non-members stand in the way of progress. Fortunately, in most groups this belief is never acted upon: the members simply hold themselves smugly aloof from outsiders, who are considered deluded, stupid or sinful.

A few authoritarian groups try to destroy anyone who is not "advanced" enough to join them, or who dares to oppose them. Shoko Asahara taught members of Aum Shinrikyo to murder opponents, claiming that it would annul their victims' bad karma. He called this supposed cleansing *poa*. In the words of one follower, "when your guru orders you to take someone else's life … you are killing that person exactly at the right time and therefore letting that person have his *poa*."[82] Ed Husain pulled away from the Hizb when one of its members murdered a non-Muslim outside his London college.[83]

Ed Husain evaded the final point of closure, when opposition to the group has become so sinful that opponents have no right to exist, and even genocide seems rational to the impassioned follower. The elements of coercive control merge to grant a group the right to destroy opponents.

Loaded language is used to dismiss critics who are believed to be demon-possessed by many groups. Identity Christians, for example, regard Jews as the descendants of Satan, and dismiss African Americans as "mud people." The use of the term "imperialist" by communists or of "commie" by capitalists exemplifies this thought-stopping use of labels. With these labels, critics rescind the humanity of their opponents. After all, the only good commie (or imperialist, depending on the extremist's point of view) is a dead one.

One member cheerfully told me that his group – which was seeking charitable status at the time – had to be "fascistic" and to eradicate opposition, because otherwise the human race would die out. Time was too short to behave in an ethical way, and the law had to be disregarded, so that critics – like me – could be harassed into silence. Otherwise, so he believed, the planet would perish.

Opponents are dehumanized, so Omar Khan Sharif walked up to Mike's Place in Tel Aviv wearing an explosive belt, just a few hours after sympathizing with Israeli children maimed by earlier suicide bombers.

Omar Khan Sharif's sheikh, Omar Bakri Muhammad, openly declared that "all non-Muslims are rebel criminals against God."[84] Interviewed after Omar Khan Sharif's death, Bakri asserted, "We don't make a distinction between civilians and non-civilians, innocents and non-innocents. Only between Muslims and unbelievers. And the life of an unbeliever has no value. It has no sanctity."[85] This is utterly incompatible with the respect for other beliefs taught by the Prophet.

systematic manipulation

Most authoritarian group members turn away from the outside world, but a few turn upon it, and become terrorists, like Omar Khan Sharif and Asif Hanif. The conditions described here can be employed by a cynical manipulator to create fanatics, but they can also arise spontaneously, as we shall see in the next chapter. *Authoritarian group membership is to some extent a collaboration between the group and the member, because of the natural dynamics of human behavior and the conformity demanded by normal society.*

Omar Khan Sharif's case seems to prove that through subtle techniques an unwitting victim can be gulled, step by Machiavellian step, into full-blown fanaticism. It is easy to believe that victims are cajoled entirely against their will, but the collaborative aspect of the process is vital to our understanding if we are to immunize society. As social scientists have demonstrated, the techniques only work because the target is susceptible. The victim is often tricked into participation, but, once invoked, the dynamics of extremism are participatory. Fanaticism has biological roots that are mistakenly nurtured by society, priming the individual to collaborate with the manipulator. Both nature and nurture are inseparably involved.

The time has come to re-examine the criteria for thought reform – systematic manipulation – in the light of normal group dynamics.

recommended reading:

Singer and Lalich, *Cults in Our Midst*
Ed Husain, *The Islamist*
Robert Jay Lifton, *Thought Reform and the Psychology of Totalism: A Study of "Brainwashing" in China.*

6
belonging and susceptibility
to coercive control[86]

"All he's doing is selling fairy tales to a bunch of people who thank him for it" ~ Leap of Faith

The understanding of coercive control is complicated by our social nature and obedience-based education. We are not by nature lone creatures. From the moment of birth, we are shaped by our society's traditions and conventions, from the language we speak, to our beliefs and biases. To be outside society is to be a loner, an outcast, or, at best, an eccentric. We are certainly at our happiest when we feel that we belong to a group. We are sociable creatures and thrive on interaction, cooperation, and competition.

Exploitative persuasion or coercive control draws upon our sociable and cooperative nature. It is vital to understand both the inborn and the social drives that prepare us for collaboration with the exploiters, if we are to undo manipulation and make a society that is resilient against future manipulation.

Exploitation takes the raw material of the normal human psyche and amplifies the existing need to belong. Founding father of social science

Gustave le Bon

Gustave Le Bon said:

"By the mere fact that he forms part of an organized crowd, a man descends several rungs in the ladder of civilization. Isolated, he may be a cultivated individual; in a crowd, he is a barbarian..."[87]

Authoritarians reduce individuality to crowd membership, as Hitler proved. Many studies show that this is a natural process.

the robbers cave experiment

William Golding's chilling *Lord of the Flies* was published in 1954. That same year, as part of a psychological experiment, 22 Oklahoma City schoolboys took their holiday in the idyllic 200-acre Robbers Cave State Park.[88] Golding surmised that without adult supervision, schoolboys would revert to vicious tribalism. Pioneering psychologist Muzafer Sherif always held the Oklahoma City boys back from causing bodily harm, but there are fascinating parallels between Golding's story and this seminal experiment.[89]

The Oklahoma City boys all came from similar backgrounds – they were Protestant and middle-class, aged between 10 and 12 years. None were considered problem children. None came from broken homes. They had a similar educational level. They were separated into two groups before they met, so there was a balance according to height, weight, skill at sports, popularity, musical and performance skills, cooking and swimming. None of the boys had met before the experiment.

During the first week, the groups were kept apart – not even knowing of the other group's existence. Observers acting as camp guides watched as the separate groups formed and adjusted hierarchies. All the boys wanted to seem "tough", so minor injuries were not reported until well after the event. Both groups chose a name and made a flag, labeling T-shirts and caps of their own accord. They called themselves the Eagles and the Rattlers.

On the evening of the seventh day, the Rattlers were allowed to overhear the Eagles playing baseball. One boy from the Rattlers suggested they "run off" these strangers. The atmosphere changed: boys who had been picked on were now given sympathetic treatment – a boy who cried was comforted rather than teased; a non-swimmer was encouraged and taught how to swim. Belief in an enemy group made the boys bond.

A series of contests was proposed, including tent-pitching. Earlier disinterest towards this activity now transformed into enthusiastic practice. By offering goals that required team effort, the experimenters had seen their hypothesis of group formation confirmed.

The groups laid claim to territories – such as the swimming holes and the baseball diamond – and questioned the right of the other group to use these facilities. They were eager for combat.

The groups were kept apart for another day, allowing tensions to build. As expected, each demonized the opposing team. Jeers and challenges began as soon as the boys caught sight of each other. Through subtle adjustments, the observers managed to keep the scores neck and neck throughout the contests. Hostility between the groups grew with each new activity. One Rattler called the adversaries "communists", to the hearty agreement of his friends.

The Eagles thought their luck depended on their prayers and their sense of fair play. Although they jibed as much as the Rattlers, they scorned their unsportsmanlike opponents. This did not stop them from tearing down and burning the enemy flag after the Rattlers had left the baseball pitch. The next morning, the Rattlers retaliated by grabbing the Eagles' flag, and the ensuing fistfight had to be broken up by the adult observers.

The Rattlers raided the Eagles' cabin at night, overturning beds and challenging the Eagles to battle. The conflict raged through the second week. Then the experimenters set up mutual activities, to see if this would quiet the resentment. It did not, until an external threat was proposed: the boys were told that vandals had blocked the camp's water supply. The two groups of boys worked together to repair the water tank. They helped each other to start a stalled truck. They divided tasks at a picnic. These activities continued, until group lines blurred, and, at the end of the third week, the boys voted to travel back home together, on a shared bus, with their new friends.[90]

The groups had formed spontaneously and turned outsiders into enemies without discussion. Simply putting the groups together did nothing to relieve tensions, but fusing them in a common cause – and creating an external common "enemy" – did the trick.

Muzafer Sherif revealed the simple dynamics of group involvement. These dynamics operate in groups of every type, from kindergartens to gangs and terrorist groups. A similar approach ended the dreadful gang wars in British cities towards the end of the nineteenth century, with the birth of the youth club movement.[91] It has implications for the runaway growth of US gangs – like the Crips and Bloods or the Hell's Angels – which now have tens of thousands of members working as organized crime rings, because the lessons of Robbers Cave have been largely ignored.

The Oklahoma City boys clearly showed a normal bias known as "cognitive distortion". *Loyalty often slants perception.* For instance, a 1951 football game between Dartmouth and Princeton was called the "roughest and dirtiest in the history of either school."

It led to fist-fights and broken bones. When students from the two colleges were shown footage of the game, each group sided strongly with their own team. Princeton students counted twice as many fouls by Dartmouth players as were seen by Dartmouth students.[92] More recently, a study of

Dartmouth - Princeton game, 1951

news reports in the US and Britain in the days leading up to the Iraq War shows a startling difference in orientation.[93] We can *all* distort evidence to suit our bias.

the Stanford Prison Experiment[94]

Membership in a group can transform highly intelligent people overnight, even when all concerned know they are part of an experiment. During the summer recess of 1971, Professor Philip Zimbardo staged the now-notorious Stanford Prison Experiment. Fifteen student volunteers became jailors and nine became prisoners, serving in a specifically built facility set up in the basement of Stanford University. Not one of the students asked to be a jailor, but, despite the flowering of peace and love in California, all took readily to the task.[95] Participants were carefully screened to be "normal, healthy and average on all the psychological dimensions we measured ... generally representative of middle-class, educated youth."[96]

The students slipped straight into their assigned roles. Prisoners were given numbers. They had to ask permission to smoke. Their jibes were punished. The guards on nightshift woke the prisoners every two hours for a rollcall. Prisoners had to answer with their numbers.

The guards – normal college students, every one of them initially reluctant to act as guards – enforced their rule physically, pushing and even striking their charges.[97] The guards force-fed a prisoner who refused to eat, and met rebellion by stripping the prisoners naked and depriving them of mattresses.[98] They used a fire extinguisher to spray dissenters, and ordered the prisoners to perform humiliating sexual pantomimes during roll call. The prisoners soon gave up their protest, and their initial good humor faded into sullen subservience.[99]

The first prisoner was released within 36 hours. As a protester against the Vietnam War, he had taken part in aggressive demonstrations, so his rapid psychological collapse confounded the experimenters.[100] A second young man cracked on day four.[101]

The whole experiment was cut short after just a week, because the psychological changes in both guards and prisoners had escalated to alarming proportions. Even Professor Zimbardo had become so engrossed in the experiment that he had to be persuaded to cut the study short.[102]

In 2002, the BBC commissioned a reality TV show broadcast as *The Experiment* which arrived at slightly different conclusions to the Stanford Prison Experiment. A paper written by the designers of this study accepted Zimbardo's pioneering work, but concluded that individual variables must also be taken into account: that group dynamics do not necessarily dictate tyrannical behavior. Initially, members of the BBC study, both guards and prisoners, tried to act in a collaborative fashion, but eventually the guards did become tyrannical.[103] It is also fair to say that the ethical guidelines for the BBC study limited participants in accord with their personalities, where Zimbardo had simply chosen "normal, healthy, intelligent college students".[104]

Milgram's obedience study

Philip Zimbardo was building on the work of his colleague, Stanley Milgram, whose compliance study at Yale had undermined conventional beliefs about our capacity for independent decision. Before his study, psychiatrists confidently assured Stanley Milgram that very few people – averaging 1.2% – would readily give powerful electric shocks to a complete stranger. According to these experts, normal people were incapable of this subservience. In fact, *everyone* in Milgram's studies pressed the lever, believing they were giving a stranger an electric shock as part of a "learning experiment". Sixty-five per cent went on to administer what was clearly labeled a dangerous dose of 450 volts when a wrong answer was given. The experts' estimate was turned on its head: only a small percentage of people did *not* fully comply.

The Milgram Experiment

No threats were made to Milgram's subjects. A man in a white coat simply assured them that they would cause no "permanent tissue damage" to the victim and said he accepted responsibility for the consequences.[105] Film of the experiment shows that many subjects agonized before pushing the button, but push the button they surely did.[106]

As Milgram said, "The behavior revealed in the experiments reported here is normal human behavior but revealed under conditions that show with particular clarity the danger to human survival inherent in our make-up. And what is it that we have seen? Not aggression, for there is no anger, vindictiveness or hatred in those who shocked the victim ... Something far more dangerous is revealed: the capacity for man to abandon his humanity ... as he merges his unique personality into larger institutional structures ... *It is ironic that the virtues of loyalty, discipline and self-sacrifice that we value so highly in the individual are the very properties that create destructive organizational engines of war and bind men to malevolent systems of authority.*"[107]

Milgram's study was repeated with many variations and by other experimenters. While the number of fully compliant participants did decline, the experiment shows that many people will comply with authority. This study led to a revision in ethics for psychological studies, so can no longer be replicated in its original form. It is also fair to say that it may not be applicable in every culture or every segment of the population.

cognitive dissonance

In the 1950s, Leon Festinger theorized that clear disproof often strengthens rather than weakens entrenched beliefs. Disagreement with a belief causes discomfort – or dissonance – which is all too often resolved by rejecting the new evidence rather than changing the entrenched belief. Left to reflect, individuals may accept disproof, but a group often bends information to harden existing opinions.

To test cognitive dissonance, Festinger and his collaborators soon found – and infiltrated – a group ready-made for their research. Marian Keech had dabbled in New Age practices including Theosophy through the "I Am" movement for years. Her Scientology counselor had even moved in with her. One morning, in 1954, she woke at dawn and felt impelled to write, but the writing that appeared on the page was not her own. She recognized her departed father's hand. She channeled enthusiastically, but was frustrated that the messages were garbled. Then one day, an impatient spirit shoved her father aside.

Sananda claimed to hail from the planetary system of Cerus and Clarion. In his last incarnation on earth, he revealed, he had been known as Jesus. Over the following months, Sananda urged Keech to gather her friends, to protect them from an impending cataclysm that would cleave the American continent in two and submerge much of the world beneath flood waters.[108]

Marian Keech's group, including Festinger's participant observers, waited for Sananda to come and rescue them from the doomed earth. When his mothership failed to appear, the group acted in line with Festinger's prediction. Rather than accepting the clear evidence that Sananda was a figment of Keech's over-active imagination, they were convinced that their activities in the run-up to the aborted rescue attempt had averted disaster. As Festinger had predicted, members who were not in direct contact with the core group fell away.[109]

For more than a century, the leaders of the Jehovah's Witnesses have repeatedly updated their prophesies for the end of the world, as one date after another has passed without catastrophe. One source reports that the next prediction for Armageddon is in 2033.[110] It is surprising that perhaps eight million people belong to this sect, given its many prophetic failures, but cognitive dissonance *usually* causes fervent believers to believe even more fervently when shown disproving evidence.

Cognitive dissonance is one of the most thoroughly researched theories in psychology.[111] It is deeply written into human behavior. For instance, two groups of female students were put through either a frivolous or an embarrassing initiation to join what turned out to be a rather boring sorority group. Those who had undergone the harsher, embarrassing ritual had a higher opinion of the group. The harder it is to achieve a benefit, the more the benefit is appreciated, so it seems. When children are ordered not to play with an attractive toy, those who are threatened with a harsher punishment if they do will think the toy more valuable.[112] We put a greater value on those items that cost us more – the difference between up-market and generic products in the supermarket is often no more than packaging, but *value* means far more than simply monetary cost.

social proof and group decisions

Agreement with a group is called *social proof*. We tend to comply with group rules and mores, so that we will "fit in". Social proof is supported by the simple and frequently replicated Asch experiment. A subject, who is unaware that the rest of the group are collaborating with the experimenter, joins a panel where the participants are asked to determine which two lines on a board are the same in length. Sometimes, the collaborators all agree on a false comparison. Although the line differences are obvious, some subjects change their opinion to agree with the group. Even those who stick to their disagreement will admit to self-doubt when interviewed later.[113] Because this compliance is automatic and unthinking, it is hard to overcome.[114]

Similarly, a long-term study of smokers underlines the group nature of many decisions – even those which seem personal and individual. Nicholas Christakis and James Fowler reviewed detailed records of over five thousand smokers and non-smokers between 1971 and 2003, focusing on their networks of relatives, neighbors, work colleagues, friends and even friends of friends. They found that stopping smoking was rarely an individual decision. Smokers tend to quit in groups, and those who do not stop find themselves marginalized. Christakis and Fowler found a similar effect in a study of obesity.[115] Presumably, any significant belief or behavior will follow a similar trend. Birds of a feather will, indeed, flock together.

mass hysteria

Even without anyone manipulating us, our reactions and perceptions are extremely malleable; we can be influenced by events and by the group to which we belong. In the final months of 2005, a fearful epidemic swept through schools in Chechnya. More than a hundred people from different parts of the country, mostly teenagers, were rushed to hospital with seizures, respiratory problems and fainting. Some patients were comatose; others had as many as four fits a day. Parents watched as their children writhed in agony, their complexions flushing from ghostly white to deep crimson, as they screamed in terror. Following the diagnosis of local doctors, a municipal governor went on television to insist that the Russians were poisoning Chechen children.

Toxicological analyses failed to reveal poison and not one of the patients responded to treatment for toxins. A Russian psychiatrist arrived with a coterie of toxicologists, and after examining the patients said they were suffering from "conversion disorder", more commonly known as hysteria.

Chechen clinical psychologist Professor Khapta Akhmedova, who had followed the Russian psychiatrist on his rounds, disagreed with the consensus of her medical colleagues, and diagnosed "mass sociogenic illness", or mass hysteria. She reasoned that it was extremely improbable that so many people so far apart would spontaneously develop identical symptoms, unless the condition was sociogenic – an illness that affects a group.

Mothers stayed at the bedsides of their hospitalized children, determined to protect them. When one started screaming, throughout the hospital the others would follow suit, maintaining the frenzy at fever pitch. To make matters worse, a mullah told one of the girls that she was clairvoyant, and she then terrified other sufferers with dire predictions. One was told that she must stab the other girls to save herself from being murdered. Another was told she would commit suicide, and, sure enough, she tried to jump from a balcony, making a second attempt soon afterwards.

Professor Akhmedova had to calm the panic. She went from ward to ward, asking the girls and their mothers to describe the events leading up to their illness. Realizing that talking was over-exciting the patients, she asked them to represent their illness in drawings, and then explain to her what they had drawn. The patients began to calm down. As soon as possible, patients were sent home to stop the contaminating effect of the group.

Akhmedova enlisted the aid of her former students, and they spent months working their way through all of the patients. As she was the only psychologist in Chechnya qualified to give cognitive behavioral therapy, she had to complete every case herself, with hours of individual attention. Through this therapy, all of the patients were eventually able to understand the true nature of their sickness. By the end of 2007, every one of them had recovered. Professor Akhmedova is convinced that at the root of the problem is the stress caused by more than a decade of warfare.[116]

Mass sociogenic illness is the most extreme expression of group dynamics. It lies at the root of witch-hunts and the wholesale persecution of minorities.[117] It is important to note that even without an external authority consciously directing their perceptions and emotions through deliberate influence, entire communities can share the same psychosomatic, but physically very real, afflictions. Simply by belonging to a community that shares the same culture and environment, individuals can be possessed by the same irrational fears. At its worst extreme, such group delusion creates the conditions for genocide.

In an excellent review of the literature, Robert Bartholomew and Simon Wessely concluded: "It seems clear that there is no particular predisposition to mass sociogenic illness and it is a behavioral reaction that anyone can show in the right circumstances ... *No one is immune from mass sociogenic illness because humans continually construct reality and the perceived danger needs only to be plausible in order to gain acceptance within a particular group and generate anxiety.*"[118]

Compliance with authority has another dimension – groupthink – that we shall now explore in more detail.

recommended reading:

Aldous Huxley, *The Devils of Loudon*
Arthur Miller, *The Crucible*

7
groupthink

"We are not talking about mere instinctive conformity ... What we are talking about is a rationalized conformity – an open, articulate philosophy which holds that group values are not only expedient but right and good as well." ~ William H. Whyte, 1952

Irving Janis applied the term "groupthink" to behavior that leads to catastrophes such as the Bay of Pigs fiasco.[119] In 1961, ninety days after John F Kennedy became President, a force of 1400 landed on Cuba to seize power back from Fidel Castro's communist regime. They faced an army of 200,000 with the single most popular leader in the world (according to a US Intelligence survey). This half-baked attack risked intervention by the Soviet Union and a potential Third World War, yet JFK's close advisors later told Janis they had kept alarming details from the President, to avoid upsetting him. They seemed to believe that Kennedy's charisma alone would carry them through this crazy escapade.

Of groupthink, Janis said, "Each individual in the group feels himself to be

Invaders taken prisoner at the Bay of Pigs

under an injunction to avoid making penetrating criticisms that might bring on a clash with fellow members and destroy the unity of the group ... Each member avoids interfering with an emerging consensus by assuring himself that the opposing arguments he had in mind must be erroneous or that his misgivings are too unimportant to be worth mentioning."[120]

Imitation is an important learning skill, but *unthinking* imitation turns to copycat behavior. David Phillips showed that the suicide rate increases after sensational reports of a suicide. Both the World Health Organization and the American Psychiatric Association have supported his findings. There are many recorded examples. For instance, after the 9/11 attacks, there was a spate of plane crashes into buildings around the world.[121]

dislocation and transition

Dislocation or transition paves the way for thought reform. As we have seen, psychiatrist Marc Sageman's study of 165 Al-Qaeda members showed that 78% were emigrants or living away from home when they became terrorists.[122] The process of dislocation predisposes people to changes in belief and lifestyle. Rigid habits melt into a flux, just as a caterpillar melts and reforms in the cocoon.[123] Even in the second generation, immigrants can feel that they do not belong, so they search restlessly for an identity. Adolescents are most vulnerable, because they are in a between-world of rapid change, brain transformation, heightened sensitivity and rejection of childhood values. This is exaggerated in a complex, multicultural society, because traditional paths to adulthood are either no longer followed or no longer valued.

Like Omar Khan Sharif's father, many immigrant Muslims become less involved with their religion, and their offspring's fanaticism is a rebellion rather than the continuation of an invasive foreign culture, as is often believed. Some adolescents fail to find a niche. They feel adrift, desperately seeking a deeper meaning than the narcissistic grab-it-now consumerism that seems to dominate our society.

The need to belong lures us into the manipulator's lair. The first step is often freely made, because the true intention of the manipulator is carefully concealed. *No one joins an authoritarian group begging to be exploited and demeaned.*

They join because they want to belong, because they have been flattered – often "love-bombed" – and because inflated promises have been made, whether of earthly success or heavenly illumination. After the bait of those promises, the hook comes through intense experiences that lead to extreme emotion and a lapse in reasoning – even for the most intelligent of people.

control of the social environment

Robert Jay Lifton defined milieu control as "the control of human communication", saying that the totalist individual seeks to control not only communication with the outside world but "over what we may speak of as his communication with himself."[124] This is the information control aspect of Steven Hassan's BITE model taken to its last extreme.

Removed from their daily environment, the boys in the Robbers Cave study immediately conformed their behavior to the group. The same is true for the students in the Stanford Prison Experiment. Little indoctrination or additional pressure was needed. Students slipped into the uniforms of either guard or prisoner and instantly fitted the role they had been assigned.

As Asch's *social proof* experiment shows, individual certainty may quietly crumple in a group of strangers. Omar Khan Sharif was caught up entirely with al-Mujahiroun. His outside interests faded, including his university study, employment and, eventually, even his own small children, whom he abandoned to become a "martyr".

Thankfully, social proof depends upon the society itself. When Perrin and Spencer replicated the line experiment in 1979 with 396 science students, conformity only occurred in one instance. A 1996 meta-analysis of 133 studies showed that conformity seemed to have declined in the years following the original study.[125] This gives us hope that less authoritarian societies will be more resistant to groupthink.

informal control

Control of behavior, information, thought and emotion can also occur informally. In the environment provided, the Stanford students adopted what they believed to be the behavior of guards or of prisoners.

A study of news reports in the US and Britain in the lead up to the Iraq War shows a startling difference in orientation. This aligned with massive protest in Britain, and a fervor for war in the US. Many people still believe that Iraq was implicated in 9/11, because of false media reports.[126] While Saddam Hussein was a despicable tyrant, there is no evidence that he supported Al Qaeda's appalling attacks on the US.

In an extremist group, time can be completely controlled – which also controls behavior – but even slight restrictions on time can have a significant effect. Three groups of students were told they were either running late, just on time, or had time to spare before setting off to give a talk. On the way, they passed a man slumped in a doorway who moaned and coughed twice. The majority of those with time to spare spoke to the man, almost half of those who were just on time spoke to him, but only a tenth of those who were late stopped. Several of this last group actually stepped over the man to get to their talk. The irony is that participants were Christian seminary students, and the talk they were rushing to give was about the Good Samaritan.[127]

authority

Stanley Milgram showed how easily authority can be projected onto a man in a white coat. Most of his subjects simply followed orders and accepted that the responsibility for their actions belonged to the experimenter. The War Crimes Tribunal at Nuremburg rejected this excuse – *befehl ist befehl* ("orders are orders"). According to this precedent in international law, even if we commit an immoral act in support of our nation's law, we are still fully responsible for that act. Reflecting on his study, Milgram said, "Even Eichmann was sickened when he toured the concentration camps, but he had only to sit at a desk and shuffle papers. At the same time the man in the camp who actually dropped Cyclon-b into the gas chambers

Hermann Goering and fellow Nazis on trial at Nuremberg

was able to justify *his* behavior on the ground that he was only following orders from above ... the person who assumes responsibility has evaporated. Perhaps this is the most common characteristic of socially organized evil in modern society."[128]

The essential aspect of Robert Jay Lifton's loaded language is that it inhibits thought and prevents discussion through "thought terminating clichés."[129]

Loaded language, indeed, any esoteric language, conveys authority, because we are not taught to be skeptical of the special knowledge it implies, and, typically, authority-figures are impatient with questions. Language is shaken free of its definition to imply unspoken connotations. There is justification for the use of precise technical terms, but mere pretense of science is usually buttressed by elaborate language.

Subjects in the Milgram experiment volunteered for a "study" where each became a "teacher" giving electric shocks to a "learner" under the supervision of an "experimenter". The language alone prepared them for obedience in the name of Science.

In *Nineteen Eighty-Four*, George Orwell suggested that language could be restructured to prevent the possibility of negative feeling toward the state, because words for such *thoughtcrime* would no longer exist.[130]

Abstract notions such as "freedom" are loaded with emotion in our society and it becomes almost blasphemous to question their definition. Hitler fired up his followers by packaging complex historical themes into simple expressions, such as "blood and soil" or "living space", circumventing the possibility of discussion.

Robert Jay Lifton readily admitted that loaded language "exists to some degree within any cultural or organizational group, and all systems of belief depend upon it. It is part of an expression of unity and exclusiveness," but added, "The loading is much more extreme in ideological totalism, however, since the jargon expresses the claimed certitudes of the sacred science."[131] Even so, thought-terminating clichés are part and parcel of contemporary life, especially in war. Allies are killed by "friendly fire" and innocent victims become "collateral damage." In this way, they are deprived of humanity and transformed into objects that can be turned into statistics without emotional concern.

In both Stanley Milgram's study and the Stanford Prison Experiment, adults gave up their power without reservation. Margaret Singer rightly comments on the deliberate removal of power, but the first part of that process is often an *abdication* of power, because of habitual submission to authority, or, in some cases, a habitual opposition to authority. In this last case, people join a group because of that opposition, without realizing that they are now actually submitting to a new authority.

Only a sociopath is without shame. The rest of us feel relief when we admit our mistakes. Religions and psychotherapies alike encourage confession. In stressful situations, or under the influence of alcohol, some people make spontaneous admissions to virtual strangers. The bad cop/good cop method of interrogation often leads to spontaneous confession, too. It is not necessary to encourage some people to "confess;" I have often heard intimate details from strangers while travelling on a plane or train. And, in spite of "client confidentiality," many lawyers, doctors and therapists tell their clients' stories, believing that they have not violated confidentiality, simply because they do not name the client. The ground is well prepared for an exploiter to abuse the trust placed in confession.

demand for purity

Lifton's demand for purity is inbuilt. We feel guilty when we break the rules of our particular society. Guilt manipulation is easy, once you know those societal rules, and once invoked it is self-enforced. According to Lifton:

"Each person is made vulnerable through his profound inner sensitivities to his own limitations and to his unfulfilled potential..."[32]

That sensitivity exists as an aspect of normal enculturation. Everyone is raised within a moral framework that will in some ways be different to other groups. Prohibitions against criminal and immoral acts are part of the fabric of any society. Some words are considered rude or profane, and their use can induce guilt in the speaker or, conversely, an urge to correct the speaker. Many people have an involuntary response to "swear" words, which can be measured in a brain scan. Both "snarl" and "purr" words create automatic responses. There are also conventions for both behavior and appearance that stimulate automatic responses.

The boys at Robbers Cave kept minor injuries to themselves, because their upbringing made them feel that it was cowardly to complain. Kennedy's advisers kept reservations to themselves, as if to maintain the unsullied purity of the Camelot ethos.

The demand for purity builds upon simple conditioned conventions, but, as Lifton says, puts them beyond reach. If these conventions were not taken so seriously, the demand for purity would have nowhere to lodge.

Through centuries of religious intolerance in Europe, whole societies shared the same inflexible culture. Dissent in even a small detail led to torture and even execution as a heretic or a witch. Kingdoms waged war over doctrinal differences. In these days of pluralism, we tolerate a broad range of practices, but certain values distinguish contemporary western culture.

There is an old adage that in the country of the blind, the one-

eyed man is king, but as H. G. Wells pointed out, in the country of the blind, the one-eyed man is more likely a despised outcast.[133]

the mystical imperative

The demand for purity extends to the *mystical imperative*. Only through purification will the individual become worthy of the profound insights that the group promises. Until that insight dawns, the follower must obey the higher authority of the group and persuade others to accept that authority. Whether we grant authority beyond our own understanding to supernatural forces, to the superior information of scientists, or to political leaders, is not the issue. When they rely on higher authority, people sometimes do not even understand what they preach, but the sense of community can induce a wonderful emotional experience for all concerned.

Under the mystical imperative, a goal is set to achieve utopia in this world or the next, or to achieve a harmony with the universe through "enlightenment", or simply to resolve the pain or distress of everyday life.

Participants in the Robbers Cave, Yale and Stanford studies all showed a readiness to accept an imperative set by a higher authority. Membership of a group inclines people towards groupthink. Once a leader has gained our support, we will follow them to hell and back. So it was that the overthrow of Castro became a mystical imperative for the Kennedy administration, which cast reason to the winds to pursue this impossible goal.

Lifton defines the exaggeration of normal loyalty in his *psychology of the pawn*: "Feeling himself unable to escape from forces more powerful than himself, he subordinates everything to adapting himself to them ... his psychological energies merge with the tide rather than turn painfully against himself. This requires that he participate actively in the manipulation of others ... he has been deprived of the opportunity to exercise his capacities for self-expression and independent action."[134]

This pawn psychology is found in everyday religious and patriotic fervor. The qualities of faith and trust necessary for submission to a mystical imperative already exist in the majority of people.

The capacity to reframe experienced events to suit the ideas of experts – doctors, lawyers, scientists or religious leaders – can be very alarming. Many of Milgram's participants left their experience and their compassion at the door, deferring to the "expert" experimenter. The students turned jailers at Stanford easily swept aside their hippie ethos of peace and love to brutalize their prisoners; they needed no outsider to manipulate their guilt. It became a matter of conscience to conform to their *own* internal expectations. As one guard put it: "My enjoyment in harassing and punishing prisoners was quite unnatural for me because I tend to think of myself as being sympathetic to the injured, especially animals."[135]

In his analysis of the Nazi doctors, who willingly murdered a third of a million disabled patients, Lifton pointed to the "doubling" of identity, where an otherwise caring individual will create a separate identity to commit atrocious acts.[136] As Mick Jagger sang, "the gangster looks so frightening, with his Luger in his hand, but when he gets home to his children he's a family man."[137]

cognitive dissonance

As the theory of cognitive dissonance shows, self-justification prompts people to shape the world to their opinions. Confirming evidence is promoted, and contradicting evidence dismissed; even if fact has to be altered and memories changed to maintain certainty.

The uncomfortable feeling of cognitive dissonance can be calmed by conforming behavior to belief. Past behavior becomes too important to renounce. There is a feeling of inertia in convinced belief that makes it very hard to alter a committed course. Commitment is consistent with the resources already invested and the loss of face in changing the belief. The belief is specific enough for real world events to stand in contradiction to it – Lifton's *ideology over experience*, also called *doctrine over person*.

When a believer is then confronted with disconfirming evidence, a lone individual will often change the belief, but a group member will fall back upon the group to dismiss even the hardest of evidence. So, against reason, cultic and irrational beliefs are often strengthened by contradicting evidence[138] (unless the contradiction comes from the authoritarian leader's own pronouncements, when it *sometimes* undermines faith in that leader). When the mothership did not come, Sananda's handful of earthly followers convinced themselves that they had somehow saved humanity without even knowing how.

Lifton's eight criteria of thought reform:
- milieu control
- loading the language

- mystical manipulation
- sacred science
- demand for purity
- confession
- doctrine over person
- dispensing of existence

doctrine over person

Doctrine over person reduces outsiders to bloodless stereotypes and leads to *dispensing of existence*. The Stanford guards numbered the prisoners, taking away their individuality along with their names. The first inclination of the Rattlers was to run the Eagles off, rather than befriend them. Most of Milgram's participants stripped the subject of his humanity, because of the supposed importance of an "experiment".

The record is altered to fit the doctrine —the *experience* to fit the *ideology*. Under the Stalinist regime, heroes of the revolution who had fallen foul of the dictator were removed from history. Librarians systematically rubbed their faces out of publications.[139] Anyone who mentioned their achievements was scorned, so they were lost to public memory: the doctrine of communism was more important than the truth. Even the great composer Dmitri Shostakovich was publicly humiliated for failing to write music in the proper socialist form. He might easily have lost his life to Stalin's caprice.[140]

Lifton, speaking of the Chinese Communist thought reform program, said: "The totalist milieu [environment] maintains an aura of sacredness around its basic dogma, holding it out as an ultimate moral vision for the ordering of existence. This sacredness is evident in the prohibition ... against the questioning of basic assumptions, and in the reverence which is demanded for the originators of the Word, the present bearers of the Word, and the Word itself. While thus transcending ordinary concerns of logic, however, the milieu at the same time makes an exaggerated claim of airtight logic, of absolute "scientific" precision."[141]

sacred science

With *sacred science* comes a refusal even to consider evidence, because of an existing unshakeable, dogmatic belief. Opinions are held on to as tenaciously as addictions. As long ago as 1620, Francis Lord Bacon wrote, "The human understanding, once it has adopted opinions, either because they were already accepted and believed, or because it likes them, draws everything else to support and agree with them."[142] Doctrine is beyond question, because it is seen as either holy writ or scientific fact – or both. Even in the "normal" world, people often accept information without proof, because it comes from a religious authority or a qualified scientist.

The contemporary misinterpretation of *jihad* – literally "struggle" – fuels terrorist fanaticism. Religious belief has all too often led to inhumanity; similarly, claims to scientific authority can also derail good sense. The scientific method is invaluable, precisely because it demands skepticism rather than slavish devotion, even towards those with the best scientific credentials. Yet even scientists can base opinions on accepted dogma or ideology, rather than on the evaluation of evidence, or experience.

As recently as the 1980s, medical scientists the world over dismissed Dr. Barry Marshall's claim that stomach ulcers are caused by a bacterium, because "scientific" textbooks said that bacteria *cannot* live in the stomach. It took a decade before his empirical proofs were accepted and doctors began to treat ulcers – very successfully – according to those proofs, putting aside the unquestionable assumptions of a sacred science. In fact, some ninety-five per cent of stomach ulcers are caused by *helicobacter pylori*. Barry Marshall and his tutor Robin Warren received the Nobel Prize for medicine in 2005.

the slow pace of paradigm shift

There is an alarming tendency for even highly intelligent people to hold tight to the conventions they learned in their earlier years. In the 17th century, William Harvey reasoned that the blood flows through the body, pumped by the heart, dismissing the first century physician Galen's notion that the blood flows in tides. Harvey was reviled by doctors and the expression "it is better to err with Galen than to be right with Harvey" came into use. We are creatures of habit, even the brightest of us, so it often takes a generation for a dearly held belief to change. This change of deeply held belief is called "paradigm shift."[143]

The Bay of Pigs exemplifies the attitude of inviolable doctrine that characterizes sacred science. The invasion was beyond question, because it rested upon a moral assumption – President Woodrow Wilson's oft-repeated slogan that the US must make the world "safe for democracy". The means could not be questioned, because the cause was holy. In reality, the means and the ends must always be at one with each other.

Once predisposition to manipulation is added to the mix, Lifton's model becomes a flow chart of the interaction between thought reformer and subject. At the bleak final stage of this dynamic process comes contempt for all outsiders, and the willingness to dispense with their existence, which at its most extreme becomes genocidal. A group of fanatics, such as the Japanese authoritarian group Aum Shinrikyo or the Nazis, transmutes its hatred into mass murder. However, there is no need for an elaborate thought reform program to convince soldiers to kill the enemy in times of war.

dispensing of existence

Whole societies have been driven into the *dispensing of existence*, through their contempt for other cultures and their belief in their own racial superiority. Perpetrators say that their victims are *less* than human. A Japanese officer who participated in the massacre of more than a quarter of a million Chinese at Nanking said it was a mistake to think of the Chinese as people,

The dispensing of existence through propaganda

Interwar French anti-Semitic propaganda

US WWII propaganda poster

because they were actually "swine". Allied commander General Sir Thomas Blamey told his troops that they need have no compunction in killing the Japanese because they were "subhuman beasts ... a cross between humans and apes."[144] Meanwhile, Commander-in-Chief in Iraq General Sanchez said that detainees were "like dogs".[145]

It is possible to analyze the Nazi Holocaust, the Stalinist purges, or any of the many historically accessible mass murders through the lens of Lifton's thought reform criteria, but it is important to understand that even supposedly civilized people have supported mass murder, without either external pressure or any program of coercive control.

Hitler's determination to sterilize or murder his way to a "pure" society was common to the intellectuals of his generation. In a 1908 letter, D.H. Lawrence said, "If I had my way, I'd build a lethal chamber as big as the Crystal Palace with a military band playing softly and a cinematograph working brightly. Then I'd go out in the back streets and the main streets and bring them in – all the sick, the halt and the maimed. I would lead them gently and they would smile me a weary thanks, and the band would softly bubble out the Hallelujah Chorus."

Playwright George Bernard Shaw believed that the socialist society of which he dreamed could only be achieved through active eugenics: "Extermination must be put on a scientific basis if it is to be done humanely as well as thoroughly. If we want a certain type of civilization and culture, we must exterminate the people who don't fit in."[146]

Such a chilling thought: "we must exterminate the people who don't fit in." But who is wise enough to make such a determination, and do we not lose our humanity, just as Shaw did his, if we are arrogant enough to judge whole classes of our fellow humans "unfit" and "exterminate" them?

Hitler was so devastatingly successful because he reached into the depths of the normal human psyche. He realized that society does not simply contain authoritarian groups, but is almost always an authoritarian group in itself.

In the midst of crisis, Hitler's dehumanizing message appealed to both high and low. Throughout Germany, medical doctors carried out a program of extermination on almost a third of a million disabled citizens. More than 70,000 were murdered before Hitler launched his military campaign, and long before the death camps. Forty-five percent of German medical doctors – some 38,000 – joined the Nazi Party. They were more highly represented in the party and in the SS than any other profession.[147] However, this program was based upon mass sterilization that had already occurred in California,

I am a burden to myself and the State. Should I be allowed to propogate?

I must drink alcohol to sustain life.

Shall I transfer the craving to others?

Would the prisons and asylums be filled if my kind had no children?

I cannot read this Sign.

By what right have I children?

Eugenics supporters in the USA
(placards re-typed for legibility)

with the approval of both Christian and Jewish religious leaders.[148]

methods of coercive control

As we have seen, Robert Jay Lifton defined milieu control as "the control of human communication", adding that the totalist seeks to control not only communication with the outside world, but also the individual's communication with him or herself.[149]

We can simply fall in with a perceived authority's whim, even when that authority is based solely upon status or rank, rather than expertise. Belief in authority can stop us from bothering to think.

The methods of coercive control activate reciprocal behaviors that lie dormant in almost everyone. Perhaps in *everyone* – even thee and me. Lifton's model helps us to understand how morality and reasoning may be swamped by dark emotional forces. The manipulator exploits the biological group instinct and an obedience to authority, conditioned since infancy. The individual feels a sense of community and an elevated emotional state, which in an authoritarian group is heightened through a mix of sleep deprivation, inadequate nutrition, persistent emotional arousal, and hypnotic fixation.

Individual responsibility is subsumed into a ravening group psyche under the direction of a manipulative totalist, but it is because of an existing susceptibility. Fortunately, education can greatly reduce that susceptibility.

Sometimes, individuals are turned against society without joining any group. For them, as we shall now see, a text becomes the guru and unquestionable in its authority.

recommended reading:

Robert Jay Lifton, *Thought Reform and the Psychology of Totalism: A Study of "Brainwashing" in China*
George Orwell, *Nineteen Eighty-Four*

8

coercive control at work

"As soon as one's convictions become unshakeable, evidence ceases to be relevant – except as a means to convert the unbelievers. Factual inaccuracies … are excusable in the light of the Higher Truth." ~ P.H. Hoebens

A study of extreme groups can leave the impression that they transform innocent, vulnerable people into predators – or even robots. This is simply untrue. No matter how much influence they have been subjected to, people retain enough sense of self to recover. Professor Alan Scheflin has called this the Myth of Irreversible Mind Control.

Some individuals need no group; an ideology suffices. The text takes the place of a guru. Timothy McVeigh, who killed 168 people in the Oklahoma City bombing, is a graphic example.

Although McVeigh shared the views of racist, right-wing groups and stayed in touch with them, he remained an outsider. He was so strongly motivated by a single book that he sold boxfuls, for cost-price, at gun fairs. But the book did not pretend to be a scripture or even a treatise. It was a novel, *The Turner Diaries*, a horrificly violent diatribe written by American Nazi William Pierce, based on the bizarre idea that the US is secretly run by Zionists.

Cultic convictions have no need for a charismatic leader. *A text can fill the place of a guru.*[150] This seems to be especially the case with Al-Qaeda.

Al-Qaeda means simply "the base". It was only after 9/11 that the name came to represent four loosely connected groups, which did not actually share central command. The world's media created the image of an enormous international conspiracy.[151] In fact, the four groups within Al-Qaeda had less than five hundred members when the World Trade Center was so viciously attacked. The massive military response, in Afghanistan and Iraq (resulting in almost a million deaths), created a backlash of support for Al-Qaeda that spread its extreme beliefs to a multitude, and is directly responsible for the rise of ISIS (or Daesh).

Even now, Al-Qaeda remains a loose association of collaborating groups, rather than a monolithic organization. It draws power from this structure. Like the Internet, it is a non-hierarchical network[152] – it has no center and can continue to exist as long as any of its separate cells (or *hubs*, in Net terminology) survives. It also recruits without direct contact: charisma is in the mind of the beholder.[153] In Al-Qaeda, as in any other authoritarian group, few followers have any significant contact with the leader, who can thus fulfill a fantasy of the perfect hero.

Young, alienated Muslims are drawn by the idea of sacrificing their lives for their religion. They are easily fired up by the preaching of fanatics, and abandon reason for the usual cultish polarized, black-and-white view of the world. They see their critics either as naive or evil.

The pre-conditions for recruitment into an authoritarian group are rife in contemporary society, so much so that many people seek out a group to join. Almost all Al-Qaeda members found the group, rather than being actively recruited. In fact, Al-Qaeda turns away most of those who wish to join – including Omar Khan Sharif.

The authoritarian only needs to amplify the normal conformist processes of society: obedience and groupthink. These processes in turn depend upon our inborn social nature.

As the saying goes, one man's terrorist is another man's freedom fighter: at the end of the 18th century, the British saw the American revolutionaries as rebels who refused to pay their share for the war that had protected them against the French, and then joined forces with that enemy. The revolutionaries insisted that they should be represented in the government of their own affairs. Young Islamists see themselves in a similar light to those revolutionaries. Causes differ, but the passionate intensity is the same.[154] We desperately need to find non-violent and just solutions.

the evolution of love

In his insightful presentation, *the Theory of Belief and Fervor*,[155] Yuval

Laor explores the different forms of love that have evolved in our species. Without them, human civilization would be very different, but these forms of love can be hijacked and abused by predatory people. So, the child's dependent love for the parent can be transferred to a leader, who may be a tyrant; the unshakable love a parent has for a child can be directed towards a group, which may take advantage of its followers; the love a teenager has for parents can be transformed into rebellion against authority; and romantic infatuation, or limerence, can create euphoria outside of romantic situations, causing an almost drug-like dependency on a toxic partner or group.

This transfer of our inborn forms of love has been significantly expanded by language. Language allows us to abstract our feelings and develop an attachment to a sports team, a faith, a nation, or, indeed, any cause or group. This power of abstraction can have benefits in mobilizing action, but it is also easily manipulated to create division and hatred or to isolate people.

A sense of certainty which is not based purely on reason is fundamental to our behavior, so much so that we are usually unaware just how much our judgement can be affected by language and by our existing beliefs. *We readily accept information that agrees with our beliefs, but often automatically dismiss information we find disagreeable.* Our emotional attachment can interfere with our ability to calmly consider evidence.

We pursue infatuation – the buzz of a new product or relationship – anything novel and pleasing. Some leaders renew that infatuated affection with specific techniques that cause euphoria or create stress and insecurity: through rallies and rituals they create a feedback loop, where followers seek to repeat earlier euphoric states, or a retreat into a sense of comfort and safety. This peak experience creates commitment to the group or partner, and the feedback loop can maintain a fervent attachment to leaders, beliefs, groups and toxic partners.

the consequences of coercive control

Involvement in an authoritarian group or relationship leaves a mark. I was lucky: my own involvement in Scientology was relatively trauma-free. I was never a live-in member, so I wasn't sleep-deprived, humiliated or bullied. Although I was a true believer, I was never a "total convert". Many people are not so lucky. I just handed over cash to learn how to apply and be subjected to processes that induce euphoria and commitment. It was disorienting, and it took me some time to recover, but I did not have post-traumatic stress disorder, as so many former members do.

I have a particular sympathy for members born into a group. Their development can be inhibited by the impossible demands placed upon them by a high-control group and the lack of opportunities to develop socially and intellectually. The same can be true for someone born into an abusive family.

The most valuable tool to overcome the effects of authoritarianism is education. I've been involved in the recovery of more than 600 former members of authoritarian groups, and most recover rapidly once they have a framework to understand the psychological aspects of the group. However, some remain stuck in the group's negative and destructive doctrines for decades after leaving the group. As Leah Remini says, "You can take the girl out of Scientology, but it's much, much harder to take Scientology out of the girl."[156]

Even with a thorough understanding of the methodology of control, many still suffer from post-traumatic stress and may need counseling. Sadly, very few counselors understand group dynamics well enough to help. Indeed, standard counseling methods can be harmful. In part, this is because before counseling can be effective, the "cultic shell" must be penetrated. The false identity implanted by a toxic group, family, or partner needs to be overcome and integrated before counseling will help. A counselor may use a method similar to the group's approach, and they may also insist on childhood trauma or changing cognitive processes without understanding that the group experience must first be addressed.

Counseling former members needs not only an understanding of the principles and practices of coercive control, but also a specific understanding of the group in question. All counseling should be a road to emotional autonomy; sometimes, counselors impose their own values rather than allowing the client to develop at their own pace and arrive at their own conclusions.

After exposure to hypnotic and non-verbal techniques, former members may have negative responses to hypnotherapy or non-verbal approaches. Some groups use extensive confession, so debriefing or journaling can stir up hurt. It is important to tailor the counseling approach to the immediate needs of the individual and to allow them to make their own discoveries at a rate of progress that suits them.

the inner identity

Group dynamics provide a basis for exploitation. There are positive methods that powerfully reduce the impact of exploitation, but without an understanding of our clannish and tribal behavior, those methods have little effect.

While everyday experience prepares the way for manipulation, the final catalyzing event often fails to occur. People do not normally spontaneously generate a new inner identity – a transformed sense of self, or a sense of the self transformed. And what exactly is "inner identity"? Is it simply an amalgam of genetic predisposition and social conditioning?

The inner identity – the self or ego – is a gradually evolving continuum. Even the religious view of a "soul" is not of an unchanging self: transformation can occur. The inner identity can be significantly redirected by trauma or revelation, but to what extent is the self simply a shape formed by external pressures, rather than a self-constructing, individual, thoughtful being?

The philosopher Nietzsche argued that "consciousness is really only a net of communication between human beings … consciousness does not really belong to man's individual existence but rather to his social or herd nature."

Studies in psychology and discoveries in neuroscience have had a profound effect on the understanding of the mind and the nature of compliance. We must now explore the human mind and the nature of consciousness more deeply, to better understand our susceptibility to manipulation.

recommended reading:

Sherif, Sherif, Harvey, White, Hood, *Intergroup Conflict and Cooperation: The Robbers Cave Experiment*
Philip Zimbardo, *The Lucifer Effect: How good people turn evil*
Stanley Milgram, *Obedience to Authority*
Festinger, Riecken, Schacter, *When Prophecy Fails*
Janja Lalich, *Bounded Choice*
Lalich and McLaren, *Escaping Utopia*

9

the mind's "I": consciousness and identity[157]

"Although many of us may think of ourselves as thinking creatures that feel, biologically we are feeling creatures that think." ~ Professor Jill Bolte Taylor, neuroscientist[158]

In 1985, the Boston Church of Christ asked Flavil Yeakley, a personality test expert, to make a study of its members. Critics insisted that the group caused unhealthy transformations of personality on its members. The Boston Church of Christ was accused of being a "cult" that was "brainwashing" followers.

Over 900 members filled in extensive questionnaires. Yeakley also administered the Meyers-Briggs' Type Indicator159 to 30 members each of six groups generally regarded as "manipulative sects" – Yeakley's expression – including Scientology, The Way, the Unification Church (or Moonies), the Hare Krishna Society, Maranatha and the Children of God, and to 30 members each in five mainstream churches: Catholic, Baptist, Methodist, Lutheran and Presbyterian. The same personality test was filled out three times by most of the subjects – as if it were five years earlier; from their present perspective; and how they anticipated they would answer five years into the future.

In Yeakley's words, "Changes in psychological type do not indicate normal healthy growth. Such changes indicate some pressure in the environment that causes people to deny their true type and try to become like someone else."[160] There were no significant deviations in personality type over time among members of the five mainstream churches, but *all* of the "manipulative sects" showed significant movement, *including* the Boston Church of Christ, in direct opposition to its leader's conviction that his group was not authoritarian.

Yeakley found that there was a convergence towards a particular personality type within each manipulative sect, but that the type varied from group to group. In other words, the "manipulative sects" were changing the personalities of their members each towards its own specific type. The effect has come to be known as "cloning", and is a substantial proof that thought reform occurs in some groups.[161]

This work is supported by a study made by Paul Martin and Rod Dubrow-Marshall, who sampled 567 former members and demonstrated significant effects relating to depression, dissociation and anxiety induced by membership of an authoritarian group.[162]

personality or identity?

The term *personality* comes from the Latin word *persona*, meaning "mask". Over the centuries, it has taken on many meanings.

There is significant disagreement about the nature of personality. Some experts are convinced that the individual is naturally a multiplicity of personalities – and speak of dissociative identity disorder[163] – but it is easy to mistake changing moods for discontinuous personalities. When they are sad, people find it hard to recollect happy memories, where happy people have difficulty remembering sad memories. This does not mean that their personalities have changed, only the mood through which personality is expressed.

The personality is made up of many identities, which are adopted according to mood and to context. Who you are speaking to – a parent, a child, an employer, an employee, a waiter or a celebrity, for instance – all these factors color identity. But these identities are strands of the continuum that makes up personality. In an authoritarian relationship, all of these identities are subsumed within the mood and behavior demanded of the member.

In one experiment, two groups were shown how to cook a specific recipe. The first group was sober, the second intoxicated with alcohol. When again sober, the intoxicated group spoiled the recipe, but could cook it when they were intoxicated again! This amusing experiment reveals "state dependence": the extent to which behavior relies upon a particular state of mind, or a particular identity. It reveals the continuum of identities that form different and quite normal states of mind.

What is it about our nature that makes us so susceptible to influence? Systematic manipulation subverts the normal pattern and implants a synthetic identity. Subjected to overpowering influence, priests will criticize their religion, soldiers disavow their homeland and formerly loving family members reject their families, through the creation of a different state of mind, a *pseudo-identity*.

the brain's complexity

I read Oliver Sacks' seminal *The Man Who Mistook his Wife for a Hat* in 1984. But, tens of brain books later, I still find the mass of terminology and the extremely complex architecture of this magnificent organ somewhat overwhelming.

I have some slight grasp of the major areas of the brain and the functions within it, but I still could not differentiate the anterior cingulate cortex from the periaqueductal grey on a three-dimensional model. Or even on a two-dimensional diagram.

We should also bear in mind the philosopher Wittgenstein's caveat: "Thinking in terms of physiological processes is extremely dangerous in connection with the clarification of conceptual problems in psychology ... [It] deludes us sometimes with false difficulties, sometimes with false solutions."[164]

Let us begin with a simple idea: if the "unconscious" is Mount Everest, then consciousness is about the size of a pebble on the top. The "awareness" or "working memory" is about two to three seconds in capacity.[165] Different measures lead optimistic investigators to stretch this to perhaps 20 seconds, but no further.[166] At most, the tip of awareness through which we peer both into the world and into ourselves has seven channels of information (give or take two channels),[167] each the equivalent of three digits wide – and only the brightest and most awake among us have nine channels available. Sleep deprivation, fasting, drink and other drugs can all reduce that tip of awareness to nothing.

This does not mean that we are automata or robots, as some contemporary researchers suggest. We are able to consider our own behavior and belief, and to follow carefully laid out plans across a course of years. We can marshal our thoughts and concentrate to recover information that might be relevant and predict the immediate future.

A model called the "theater of consciousness" says that our awareness is a "global workspace" that projects a spotlight into the unconscious to retrieve information. This differs from the simple idea that the "self" is simply the brief flash of attention or "consciousness". Much of the unconscious – including our memories and beliefs – is available. There is a tendency to fall back on the idea that the unconscious is a Mr. Hyde, a dangerous "id" that lurks behind our every action. This is simply not true. Indeed, it is better to think about "unconscious processes" rather than gathering these together as an "unconscious mind".

In this case, the "theater" is distributed through the mind – rather than the duality of a self watching the theater, the self is both the theater *and* the performance inside it. The performance and the theater constantly construct each other and are inseparable. More than a century of investigation into the brain has failed to find a central control point (or soul). Each of us is a distributed being, with myriad interacting parts creating a self that changes at every moment.

It is important to note that almost every view of human behavior relies upon a fragmentation of the self. Many religions suggest inhabiting demons or a differentiation of the "soul" and the "spirit". The Hindu *Bhagavad Gita* is one of many texts that differentiate mind and spirit. Sufi mystics speak of the "commanding self" or *nafs*, which is similar to the id of Freudian mythology. The "subconscious" or "unconscious" are seen as separate entities. The "unconscious mind" is not an invisible agent directing conscious thought, but a stream of processes or behaviors that are *preconscious*. These processes are so swift that we are usually not aware of them. This does mean that we cannot be aware of them.

I am arguing against these presumptions: we are a unity of mind, body and spirit, each of us a "self". Only through brain damage or psychological disturbance does the individual self disintegrate into dissociated parts. I have adopted the term used by composer Brian Eno for this view of the self: distributed being.[168]

The extraordinary case of the man called "Zasetsky" in the writings of brain scientist Luria illustrates the nature of distributed being.[169] Zasetsky suffered serious damage to the left side of his brain during the Second World War. He spent 25 years recording his experience of the world, although he had lost the ability to recognize and name even simple objects. Every day, Zasetsky struggled to reconstruct his shattered world. His notebooks show what happens when parts of the consortium of the normal self are destroyed.

We are not simply automata, governed by unconscious processes. We do not simply react to stimuli – through education and preparation we can learn to respond more rationally. Training can marshal our unconscious processes, and bring them into accord with our decisions, our plans, our beliefs and our motivations. *The purpose of this book is to enhance the conscious response to attempts to access our unconscious processes.*

Without consciousness, we would be in a black-out, like the so-called "paralytic" drunkard. We can point our attention inwards or outwards – all seven or so channels – and when our very limited attention is fully occupied, it becomes easier to install a random instruction into that busy mind. We will explore that topic later.

Another complexity is the encoding of ideas into language. It is a serious – and frequent – mistake to believe that what we call "consciousness" is contained in words. In fact, conscious thought often precedes the words that will express it. This is well known to writers. What sems to be a simple thought occurs in a flash, but when we come to write it down it may take up a paragraph or even a page.

This concentrated form of consciousness is at work behind our words. Otherwise, we would have to take long pauses in conversation to assemble the words for even the simplest of statements.

It is worth starting out with the usual platitudes: our brain is by far the most complex mechanism known to human study. It contains perhaps 100 billion individual neurons, each of which can receive up to a thousand signals at a time.[170] It is probably necessary to read that passage several times to even begin to realize just how astonishing the potential combinations are.

I reject comparisons between computers and brains, because a digital computer has a switching system that can receive a single signal at each cell, and that signal will be either a zero or a one (a binary digit, or 'bit'). A brain cell can not only receive up to a *thousand* signals, but these signals can be electrical, chemical, or even mechanical – and a multitude of chemicals from simple elements to complex neurochemicals are involved in the signaling.

Almost any human brain has more cells than there are leaves in the Amazon rain forest and more signaling possibilities than there are atoms in the universe[171] – and it is a very, very big universe, with at least a hundred billion galaxies each averaging a hundred billion stars. My endeavor is to present a useful picture of this complexity, without drowning in scientific jargon and convolute notions.

It is also worth bearing in mind that the doctors who first labelled brain areas shared Latin as their common language (or *lingua franca*), it sounds far less academic when we realize that there are aspects of the brain called the almonds – amygdalae, others walnuts – ganglia, and, of course, the sea-horse or hippocampus.

the two halves of the self

In the early 1960s, epileptics who lived in the half-world of almost constant seizures were subjected to radical surgery. The *corpus callosum,* which connects the two halves of the brain, was severed. To the delight of the patients, the seizures stopped. To the astonishment of the doctors, however, the patients sometimes responded as if they were now two separate people sharing a single body.

If the eyes were shielded, one from the other, and one shown an apple and the other an orange, the patient would *say* an apple had been seen, but *write* that it was an orange. This had led to the view that the two halves of the brain maintain different functions.

Once the *corpus callosum* is cut, the integration between the two hemispheres ends. The left hemisphere – which controls the right side of the body – is usually the reasoning part, and the right side is the emotional and intuitive part (this reverses in left-handed people).

One hemisphere tends to dominate. Where the balance weighs too heavily, an individual can become either too emotional to be able to reason, or too calculating to understand the inevitable emotional consequences of their calculation. In common parlance, this reflects the heat of passion and the coldness of reasoning. It allows crimes of passion and crimes where passion has been completely suspended: cold-blooded murders. However, with a normal *corpus callosum,* we should view this simple division with skepticism: the hemispheres are part of a marvelously integrated system.

The picture is further complicated by the distinct areas of the brain. The old brain, limbic system, or primary cortex is the same in mammals as it is in reptiles. Wrapped around this is the secondary cortex or mammalian brain. During the evolution of apes from monkeys, the tertiary cortex developed. It is far larger in humans than in other primates. A popular adage among psychotherapists is that every client is simultaneously a crocodile, a horse and a human, because of these three distinct brain regions.

Our habits, our addictions, and our beliefs all form "neural pathways" in the brain. A pattern of neurons will fire in a particular sequence in response to the environment. Particular neural pathways are stimulated in response to certain situations. Nobel prize winner Gerald Edelman has pointed out that, in the brain, *"what fires, wires"*, so neural pathways are laid down with any new activity, and will then be followed habitually when that activity is repeated.[172]

Bee dance

First impressions are usually the strongest, and we find it very hard to override them, even when we know they are wrong. This helps to explain the difficulty even highly intelligent and knowledgeable people have in accepting new evidence. The original belief has "wired" into the brain, in Edelman's terms.

Let us consider another metaphor for neural activity: a beehive. When choosing a new location for the hive, honeybees exhibit a strange and exact form of democracy. Scouts return and attract others to their cause by the vigor of their dance; this dance will show how to navigate to their chosen spot. Other bees make their reconnaissance and will vary from apathy to enthusiasm in their own directional dance. This enthusiasm is cumulative. Some locations will attract more voters than others. Eventually, a large enough group will carry the election and the colony will move on to pastures new. Far from being a slave society, answering to the demands of the queen, bees are actually far more democratic than we humans.

It is only a metaphor, but individual bees can be compared to individual neurons in the brain, and factions to groups of neurons that begin to fire together. Eventually, the colony of brain cells in a particular decision-making area will fire together, with stragglers joining the majority. Perhaps human anxiety is a state where renegade cells continue to agitate against the majority, and insanity a state where no consensus can be maintained.

self, mind, and thought

The traditional idea that the mind contains thoughts viewed by the self – called Cartesian duality – is in retreat. Psychologists now recognize that there is no distinction between the self, the mind and the thought. The traditional terms are deceptive. Just as it is factually wrong to say that the sun "rises", so it is wrong to believe that the "self" *has* a "mind" which *contains* "thoughts".

The ancient Buddhist view of *anatta*, which says there is no self, but an ever-changing process, is taking hold in the sciences of the mind. Herman Hesse elaborated on this theme in his remarkable novel, *Steppenwolf:* "every ego, so far from being a unity is in the highest degree a manifold world, a constellated heaven, a chaos of forms, of states and stages, of inheritances and potentialities. It appears to be a necessity as imperative as eating and breathing for everyone to be forced to regard this chaos as a unity and to speak of his ego as though it were one-fold and clearly detached and fixed phenomenon. The delusion rests simply upon a false analogy. As a body everyone is single, as a soul never."[173]

Alan Watts put forward the idea that the self is comparable to a whirlpool, which retains its shape, even though the energy – the water – that creates that shape is ever-changing.[174]

There is even some suggestion that normal personality consists of interacting and distinct hierarchies in the brain. Seven hierarchies, suggested by eminent neurologist Jaak Panksepp, have been named by psychologist John Gottman – the commander-in-chief, the nest-builder, the jester, the sensualist, the explorer, the energy czar and the sentry. In Gottman's view, one or two of these characteristic behaviors dominates in an individual, although the idea does not seem to have been properly explored.[175] However we divide ourselves up, these various "identities" are part of our individuality.

Coercive control interferes with the organic development and expression of the interacting facets of individuality. Because of the intricacy of the brain, it is relatively easy to divert the normal process. A successful manipulator fosters a new identity, a *pseudo-identity*, within the victim of coercive control. Through specific techniques, authoritarians create a new identity in the believer. The identity is grafted onto the existing or "authentic" personality so constitutes a "pseudo-identity."[176] This pseudo-identity is noticeable in ordinary conversation, when the glib enthusiasm of an authoritarian believer slips and the more natural self emerges. When they leave a manipulative sect, it is usual for believers to gradually return to their earlier personality and behavior. This can take months or years. In some cases, the unwanted beliefs plague a former member for a lifetime.

The emergence of the true personality is easily prompted by focusing the individual on activities he or she enjoyed before the authoritarian took over. When a person looks at photographs that precede membership, or talks about childhood holidays, color returns to the skin, a sparkle comes back to the eyes, and the fixed grin is replaced by a natural, or *Duchenne,* smile.

This difference between identities can be very striking: on the second day of an intervention, a previously convinced authoritarian group member (an athletic young man, whose authoritarian convictions had only just begun to seep away), held out his arms in front of him as he descended the stairs and said excitedly: "My skin is pink. Yesterday it was grey!"

The pallid complexion is blushed once more with life, and the glittering, gimlet eyes often lose their urgency when an authoritarian group member speaks about life before membership. As the skin flushes with color, the pent-up, anxious energy of permanent fight-or-flight subsides. Similar effects have often been observed as subjects come out of the altered state commonly known as hypnotic trance.

The cloned pseudo-identity draws its energy from the more complete self that formed naturally over the years before the coercive control program began. After leaving a high-pressure group into which individuality was subsumed, a former member may *float* back into the world-saving urgency instilled by the group. One woman told me that when she visited a supermarket in her first week away from an authoritarian group in almost two decades, she felt a surge of pity for the blindly ignorant trolley pushers, accompanied by a dreadful fear of her separation from the group.

Another former member told me that after he left the group, he realized that his basic emotion had been anxiety verging on terror for decades, even though, for some time after leaving, he too felt superior to the purposeless and unilluminated folk all around him.

escaping an authoritarian environment

It can take years to reintegrate the synthetic pseudo-identity. The normal response on leaving an authoritarian relationship is an attempt to wall it off, because of the helplessness associated with it, rather than accepting and embracing the lessons to be learned.[177] For this reason, former members may live in a prolonged adolescence. Something similar can happen to those who have been forcibly interned in prisons or concentration camps. The power of decision has been overwhelmed. Members no longer believe in their own capacity to make choices, so seek direction from an authority figure. Institutionalization results when the right to decide has been taken away.[178]

The simple route to subverting individual control is through confusion induced during a heightened emotional state.[179] Reasoning is clouded by all extreme emotions, whether awe, rage, terror, grief or elation. These strong feelings belong to the oldest part of the brain, which bypasses deliberate thought to generate rapid response to potential dangers.[180]

Quick reactions are often a matter of life or death. The amygdalae take signals from the eyes and ears before they have travelled to the prefrontal lobes of the brain for analysis. This is the fight-or-flight response that hits or runs before there is time for reflection. In some circumstances, this is quite simply lifesaving. Without it, humanity would not have survived. But *when highly emotionally aroused, people are more controllable and less capable of rational thought.* They react rather than considering. They will afterwards use the full weight of their intellect to justify their reaction, rather than candidly examining that reaction. It is hard to change a behavior if you *cannot* see that it needs changing, so the *stupid* reaction will become habitual, and be defended by a whole edifice of "reasoning".

Constant pressure keeps the old, reptilian brain active. Heightened emotion reduces human beings to a reptilian state, where they will respond to the chemical drench of adrenaline, cortisol, and opioids caused by the fight or flight response. This has a significant effect upon mood and health. Fanatics alternate between the pumped state of adrenaline and the chilled-out state of endorphin release. They are simultaneously anxious *and* delirious. The new, more rational mammalian brain is chemically beaten into submission by these hormones.

Groups often use methods that heighten emotional susceptibility. The common denominator is conformity, where everyone in the group acts in the same way – singing, chanting or dancing together. This type of euphoria can be generated at football matches, at rock or rap concerts, or at political rallies.

Individuals briefly fuse their identity with the group and march in lock step. The wielders of manipulation want this fusion to extend into every moment of life. Release from the anxieties of individuality into the group experience can be highly beneficial, unless it becomes the sole activity of the individual – being subsumed into the greater identity of the gang, pedophile ring, terrorist group, or "firm" of sports hooligans. At worst, armies of individuals give up their judgment and morality to commit genocide.

When drenched by intense emotion, we become more compliant, less sophisticated in our thinking, and more given to unthinking obedience. We "go with the flow" more readily. The fervent rallies staged by the Nazis enlivened a nation with belief in its superiority and its thousand-year rule over other supposedly lesser peoples.[181] The endorphins released by both panic and high levels of activity have *exactly* the same effect as morphine.

Although the high of endorphins feels wonderful, any high dulls the sharpness of reasoning. Athletes and fanatics can become addicted to endorphins in the same way that junkies are addicted to heroin. An injured athlete may experience withdrawal symptoms, including depression, if no longer able to exercise. Withdrawal from cultic practices can have the same effect, leading the fanatic to believe that stopping such practices is harmful, because of the low they feel.

Hooligan in training

Worse yet, when the reasoning mind is stunned by endorphin release, it is also subject to other happy chemicals – such as dopamine and serotonin – that will reinforce the rightness they feel. All is well with the world, as long as they keep chanting, selling, and generally dancing to the leader's tune; complying, of course, with the ethos – the rigid prejudices – of the group.

how the brain is tricked

Psychological studies have repeatedly shown how easily rational thinking is bypassed. Our perceptions are limited, and we interpret the meaning of those perceptions automatically. We "fill in" reasons for events that are hard to understand. We focus on what we expect to see, or what we are *prepared* to see. This opens the door to sleight of hand tricks by magicians, hypnotists, and street con artists, as well as the hocus-pocus of demagogues, whether political or religious in their claims.

In one celebrated experiment, participants are asked to count the number of passes made in a basketball video. Focused on the passes, the majority –

about 80% of participants – fail to notice the man in a gorilla suit who walks across the court.[182] This phenomenon is dubbed "inattentional blindness."[183] It shows how highly selective our normal perception can be.

There is a boundary between what we actually see and what we fill in. If a red card is held at the periphery of vision – the back of an ordinary playing card will do – people are generally surprised that they cannot discern its color, because color vision does not extend to the edge of the visual field. The card can be clearly seen, and once its color is known it will then be seen in the right color. *It is a surprising truth that we all live in a world that is partially imagined.* Some part of every perceived reality is actually virtual. This is well-known to stage magicians, whose art depends upon directing the imaginative power of an audience.

Police in Moscow were baffled by a new crime where a con artist requested directions from a stranger before asking for his wallet. About *two thirds* of people handed over their wallet without reflection. The problem for the police is whether a crime has been committed. The problem for us all is our inborn compliance with authority: Derren Brown demonstrated this behavior in one of his TV shows.[184] He walked up to a stranger and asked for directions, at the same time urging the stranger to take a bottle of water from him. Brown created confusion by splitting the stranger's attention. Into that moment of confusion, Brown slipped the request for the subject's wallet, keys and phone. The victim of this hoax took several steps before the penny dropped. *Our attention is far more controllable than we like to believe.*

The dream state which exists in the background of the mind is vital to understanding different states of consciousness. In dreams, we do not question the accuracy of our perception, even though objects can change from one moment to the next. A baby becomes a briefcase, with no perplexity on the part of the dreamer. The sense of judgment is suspended, and we do not even question our nonsensical imaginings. This innocent belief can carry over into the waking state, so that beliefs are asserted as "knowledge" without any need for evidence.

We are bombarded by a constant flow of data, from our environment and from within our own bodies and minds. We can only focus on a fraction of it, so we are never fully aware of everything that *does* register. This is the simple basis for positive suggestion.

As we saw earlier, confusion, repetition, fixation and mimicry will all bring about hypnotic states. The hypnotist uses these techniques to control attention and brings about a collaboration where the subject "fills in" the context. This can create experiences that are every bit as believable as dreams. And we live in a world where people are eager to suspend belief. If not, we wouldn't enjoy movies, plays or stories.

We fine-tune our perception all the time: if you record a family meal, you will notice the sound of cutlery on playback, which we normally tune out while eating. This automatic capacity to focus occurs beneath perception. In the same way, the great (and the small) unwashed do not notice their own reek. We tune out our own bodily smell, which allows us to better notice any foreign odor in our environment.

Our ancestors survived for two million years on the African savannah because of such fine-tuning. We notice change, so any loud noise or sudden movement will attract our attention, and, perhaps, save us from the attack of a predator.

the fundamental attribution error

Psychologists speak of the *fundamental attribution error*, where we naturally emphasize our self-perception over our perception of others. If *I* am late, it is because of circumstances beyond my control, but if *you* are late, it is a deliberate slight. My self-perception favors me and doubts you. This sense is easily manipulated if an authoritarian takes over the self. Where members protect the authoritarian over themselves, they will make the fundamental attribution error with regard to any criticism or threat to the authoritarian. Critics are presumed to be immoral or misguided, so any evidence they offer will be ignored.

As we have seen, personality does not consist of a single identity. We present different identities in different circumstances. So, there is not just an intoxicated or a sober identity, but many identities that relate to different people and environments. We behave in different ways according to our status and our mood.

Talking to a close friend, we will use different language and different gestures than when we are talking to an employer, a child or a celebrity. This is the first dimension of identity – the vertical axis of the graph – where how we feel constitutes another dimension – the horizontal axis of the graph. *Who we are communicating with and the way we feel merge to express an identity.*

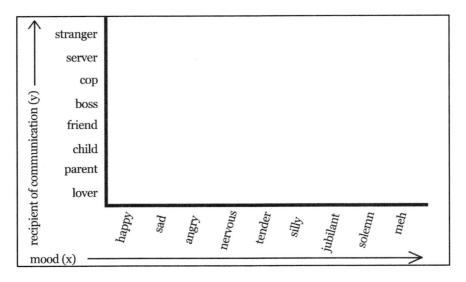

One way to see if someone is depressed is to ask for five happy memories. The truly depressed person will probably not find *any* happy memories. This does not mean that they have never experienced happiness, but that their current state of mind – the dominant identity within their personality – is unhappy.

Fanatics tend to have a restricted expression of identities. They will quite likely adopt the same language, the same tone of voice and the same gestures no matter who they are talking to. All too often, these will reflect the manipulator or follow the manipulator's demand. Scientology, for example, was created by a 100-cigarette a day smoker; it has a far higher proportion of smokers than the general population (Hubbard said that it was a fear of volcanoes in previous lives that caused smoking. His own fear of volcanoes kept him smoking until his health collapsed in his seventies).

The normal personality is a continuum of identities, which change according to circumstance. The fanatical personality exists along a far simpler continuum, and, as Flavil Yeakley found, tends to be almost *identical* in members of a particular fanatical group. The subtleties of the continuum of identities that create personality are reduced to relationship to superiors, peers and inferiors. All non-members are seen as inferiors to be recruited or shunned. In the simplest terms, the leader is the parent, fellow members are siblings, and non-members are children.

Brain disorders show the variations in identity that can occur in otherwise sane people. For instance, in Capgras Syndrome, the individual believes that friends and relations have been replaced by imposters. Otherwise, the sufferer's beliefs and behaviors are quite normal.

Alcoholics can develop Korsakoff's syndrome, where vitamin B1 deficiency leads to an inability to form new memories. The individual will still remember everything up to a certain day. They will be confused that relatives and friends have aged, because they can only remember them as they were on that day, sometimes decades before. If anyone leaves the room, the Korsakoff victim will have to be reintroduced to them when they re-enter – even moments later. Anyone at all that the sufferer did not know before the last moment of functioning memory will not be remembered, even with years of contact.

In another condition – autotopagnosia – sufferers will reject one of their own limbs, and hurl themselves out of bed, horrified that a foreign limb has been placed right next to them. In yet another, people see only the left-hand side of the world before them. There are many such conditions, which are all traceable to lesions – injuries – in a specific brain area. It is vital to understand that these people are not insane but are using their intelligence to justify their incapacity. This gives a clue to the extremes of belief found in otherwise sensible people. It is the certainty we feel in dream, no matter how crazy the events that surround us.

the placebo effect

All experiments with medical drugs have to take into account the *placebo effect*. A high proportion of people – perhaps a third – will respond to any treatment, even a sugar pill. This is not actually a deficiency. If we could fully understand such suggestibility, we could perhaps help more people to plug into their ability to heal themselves. It has been shown that there is also a *nocebo effect*: people given morphine and told that it is a saline solution may not respond to it (contrary to the "organicists" – who believe that all behavior is purely physiological).[185] This sheds light on a powerful ability of the mind and leads directly to the study of hypnosis or altered states of consciousness.

recommended reading:

Robert A. Burton, *A Skeptic's Guide to the Mind*
Merlin Donald, *A Mind So Rare*

10
the imitation game:
from copying to compliance

"Everything you are is the construction of your own thoughts." ~ The Buddhist Dhammapada

It is said that "seeing is believing", but it is quite possible to manipulate someone into believing that they have seen almost anything. This is a manipulation of the imagination. Our perception is easily directed. As we have seen, four out of five participants do not notice the gorilla-suited man who crosses the court during a basketball game, due to "inattentional blindness." We automatically focus on the task in hand to the exclusion of everything else.

It is highly relevant that in accounts of alien abduction, the subject is usually on the verge of sleep.[186] The dream nature of such experiences is apparent, because the aliens look different from one country to another – in line with local media descriptions.[187] Indeed, the first "flying saucer" was seen after a media description of a "cigar shaped" object that skimmed across the water like a "flying saucer".[188]

False memories are easily generated: in some "recovered memory" cases, therapists may well have convinced clients that they were abused in childhood.[189] As imagination and memory are shown on the same "screen" in the mind, we readily believe that an imaginary event was real, given enough persuasion.[190] When we remember and when we imagine, the relevant brain areas are activated; so, visual recall and visual imagination trigger the visual cortex. The sensation we feel will be the same in both instances.

As I have said, the dream state, which exists in the background of the mind, is vital in understanding altered states of consciousness. We experience thousands of sensations at every second – from both the outside and the inside worlds. We are constantly besieged by information, but we can only focus on a fraction of it, so we tune out the rest, without necessarily realizing that some of it may lodge without examination. This is the basis for positive suggestion, where a command by-passes consciousness.

The manipulator distracts the subject who will later find a justification for some odd, implanted behavior. A stage hypnotist may convince a subject to open a window whenever he shakes his head. The subject will protest that it is either too hot or too cold, too stuffy or too breezy, and open and close the window without realizing that these are justifications for directed actions. Eager to suspend belief, we create experiences that we believe as readily as we believe dreams while dreaming.

guided imagination

The simplest way to look at the nebulous subject of hypnosis is that the hypnotist guides the imagination. The hypnotized person *pretends* the phenomena of hypnosis, all of which occur inside the imagination, but *believes* the pretense as if it were real.

Hypnosis hijacks the normal internal process of the imagination: it is nothing more or less than guided imagining. Followers live in the pretend world of the authoritarian manipulator. Groups and even couples perform elaborate rituals that bind them together in a pretend world – a *folie á deux* or "madness shared by two people" (group belief would be a *folie á plusieurs*). We each live in our own version of the world – the world as we believe it to be – and that version can be profoundly changed by a manipulator.

Hypnosis has been a contentious subject, since Anton Mesmer introduced it to the West in the 18th century. It has been contentious for much longer in the East, where forms of it have been practiced for centuries by both Hindu *fakirs* and Islamic Sufis, who were also perhaps the first to use hypnotherapy.

Benjamin Franklin headed a French Royal Commission into Mesmer's claims. In 1784, that Commission – which also included chemist Lavoisier and inventor Guillotin – accepted that Mesmer had caused remission of illnesses, but showed that his theory of "animal magnetism" was wrong, and so mesmerism fell into disrepute.

There was a revival among Victorian doctors in the 1840s, led by Scottish surgeon James Braid, who coined the word "hypnosis", meaning a sleep state (which "hypnosis" is not). Freud studied hypnotism with Charcot in Paris, but later spoke out against its use. For most of the twentieth century hypnosis was reviled as trickery.

Hypnosis was dismissed by the dominant Behavioral school of psychology in the US, so that by the 1970s, only half a dozen out of 90 US universities included *any* material about hypnosis in psychology courses.[191] Hypnosis was considered a form of conjuring, not worthy of inclusion in a "scientific" syllabus. The view has changed markedly, although some experts still assert that hypnosis is no more than "compliance", rejecting any physiological component.

The word "hypnosis" has become so emotionally loaded that I hesitate even to use it. The same is true for "trance" or "altered state". However, better words do not as yet exist, so we must proceed with caution and without bias, if we are to understand the very real experiences and behaviors that these terms connote.

It is ironic that the words themselves conjure up fictitious suggestions: the popular notion of hypnosis is certainly a myth. It loses its sinister undertone once we understand that it is not what we believed it to be. By understanding, we become better able to resist.

This is the best technical definition I have found: "Hypnosis is a process in which one person, designated the hypnotist, offers suggestions to another person, designated the subject, for imaginative experiences entailing alterations in perception, memory and action. In the classic case, these experiences are associated with a degree of subjective conviction bordering on delusion, and an experienced involuntariness bordering on compulsion. As such, the phenomena of hypnosis reflect alterations in consciousness that take place in the context of a social interaction."[192]

Hypnosis consists of "imaginative experiences" that are guided by the hypnotist. It is worth commenting that the "hypnotist" may have no idea that the process is "hypnotic", and may believe that the brief remissions of physical and psychological conditions brought about by this approach are miraculous cures of supernatural origin.

fire-walking

We should always proceed with caution: along with "fire-walking" – where people are trained to walk over hot coals – many of the effects associated with hypnosis have been shown to be quite possible in unhypnotized subjects – for instance, it is possible to lie rigidly between two chairs or to eat an onion without any "trance" state being invoked. But despite frequent assertions that an individual will not do anything under hypnosis that they would not otherwise do, it has been shown by such hypnotists as Derren Brown that individuals can be persuaded to commit armed robbery and even murder (thankfully, with blanks in the gun) under hypnosis.[193]

"Hypnosis" and "hypnotism" refer to states induced by a hypnotist, but the hypnotist is only interacting with a human mind, which is to say, that hypnotic abilities are an aspect of the normal mind. Without this hypnotic aspect of the mind – more usually known as the imagination – we would barely be able to function.

Contrary to popular belief, hypnotic states are not induced only under special circumstances. The truth is that we all have different and special states of awareness in normal life. While reading a book, we typically separate ourselves from the world around us, and so it can be startling when someone comes into the room, because we have become "lost" in the text. In a horror film, the audience will gasp at the startling moment, although we all know that the event is only happening on the screen and was contrived by actors and employs special effects. This participation in a false reality – a shared dream – is an important aspect of hypnotic or altered states.

imagination, hypnosis and the brain

As children, we learn our times tables by repetition. The same is true for musical scales or drum rudiments. This is a positive use of the natural hypnotic aspect of the human mind. Neural pathways are formed and strengthened through repetition. After a lifetime of playing the drums, I don't have to think to play a paradiddle – which uses double and single strokes in a pattern – my hands simply play it. Asked what seven times seven is, I will answer "49" without reflection. We learn to drive, to swim, even to walk, through repetition, until the deliberate behavior becomes spontaneous. We call this "autopilot". If we try to think about those complex behaviors while performing them, we will be more likely crash the car or play a bum note or beat.

In 2016, the UK government announced that the Chinese method of repetitious learning will be used in teaching mathematics classes in the future. This is a clear, positive use of our hypnotic capacity. However, it is usually not in our best interests to simply absorb information; especially when the information comes from an untrustworthy source. Many critics of authoritarian groups believe that members are "programmed" – just as a computer is; such repetition does seem rather like programming, as it does not seek to engage the critical faculties, and may even bypass them.

Sadly, we can easily be brought to adopt behaviors that are against our own interests. An army squad or an authoritarian group can insert the direction of the leader over the individual's will. In the emergencies of war, reaction rather than reason may save lives, because hesitation can be catastrophic, but it can also lead to unthinking sacrifice and to atrocities – whether for the benefit of our fellows or because of the whim of an authoritarian leader. The same is true in any relationship where an individual is subjugated and forced to conform to the demands of an authoritarian.

awareness or working memory

Returning to the two to twenty seconds of "awareness" – or *working memory* – that is consciousness, and remembering that we can hold in mind, at best, nine chunks of information – each only three digits in width – a mechanism for hypnosis becomes apparent. These nine chunks form nine ever-changing channels. While thousands of processes continue below consciousness – breathing, the flow of blood and the many muscular movements that enable us to live, for instance – there are only, at best, nine channels of awareness to deal with both the outside *and* the inner worlds. In hypnotism, all but one channel is turned inward. The only channel into the outside world is in the control of the hypnotist.

It is a mistake to believe that a "hypnotist" is a specific personality, a Svengali with a swinging watch and a Vandyke beard. Anyone who has authority wields hypnotic power: *if we believe anyone without questioning and testing their ideas, we are to some extent hypnotized.* Nothing to do with Svengali, swinging watches or even feeling *very* sleepy. Indeed, *most* hypnosis takes place while the subject seems wide awake. But the nine channels have been narrowed, so there is no "width" to the wakefulness. In psychological terms, "exteroception" – or perception directed to the outside world – has been closed down, apart from communication from the hypnotist, who then directs "interoception": perception of our internal thoughts.

We perceive much more than we actually recognize. It is often the case that hours after a conversation the penny will drop, and we will realize what was actually said (sometimes with embarrassment). The perception and the processing of information are separate, and most of the hundred thousand words received each day from the media by a normal westerner remain un-evaluated. We absorb information without analysis, so advertising slogans and song hooks are embedded as "ear worms" without needing conscious consent.

priming

Researchers have shown the "priming" effect of the environment. We accumulate information all the time from our immediate surroundings. We often pick up unusual words from a conversation, and use them ourselves later, without noticing that we have been "primed". Images will lead us to certain thoughts. In "remote viewing", an image is made in a separate room and a "psychic" will be able to draw a similar image. However, in the conversation leading up to the event, the "psychic" will have placed an idea in the subject's mind.[194] It is clear that the remote viewer has not seen the actual picture, because, in most cases, there will be discrepancies between the images.

However, this "priming" effect is happening all the time. A hypnotist or "psychic" simply takes advantage of a natural process. Without an ability to gather up impressions from the world, artists and writers would often be without inspiration. The imagination is stimulated by the surrounding world, and those with vivid imaginations also tend to be easy subjects for formal hypnosis. They have a hypnotic *ability*, as long as they control it, rather than some unscrupulous outsider, because then it becomes a hypnotic *disability*.

It is very beneficial to take control of our own hypnotic ability (or *imagination*). It helps us to be more imaginative and to resist the tricks of the manipulators – from advertisers and spin doctors to confidence tricksters and authoritarian leaders. This has nothing whatsoever to do with self-hypnosis. Let me add that my own interest in hypnotism is purely academic – I have never taken any course in hypnosis, nor used hypnosis or hypnotherapy in my work. My interest is in the natural state rather than in a personal use of hypnosis.

Robert Jay Lifton lists the extremes of hypnotic condition in his thought reform model, where ideas are adopted from an authority that conflicts with personal experience. As we have seen, he called this "ideology over experience" or "doctrine over person".

the startle response

Our awareness – that two to three-second bubble – is easily disrupted by our startle response. Our attention can be hijacked by any sudden change. Indeed, while under stress, hypervigilance prevents full perception, like a constant startle response that makes us easier to direct and control.

Until meditator Mathieu Ricard proved otherwise, it was believed that the startle response was completely involuntary.[195] In post-traumatic stress disorder, the startle response is exaggerated. By maintaining environmental stress – loud noises (or music), bright lights, body-shaking rhythms – we can blur our sense of separation from others, be included into the collective, merge our personal bubble into the larger bubble. When we *choose* to merge, this is all well and good, but interrogators deliberately overwhelm their subjects to close down reasoning and amplify compliance.

People who have been subjected to bombardment sometimes dive to the ground at the slightest noise. In normal life, the startle response pulls attention towards a potential threat. For our species to survive, it has always been necessary to take notice of any noise, movement, or smell that is out of the ordinary. A hypnotic state relaxes that boundary perception, allowing an outsider to direct the imagination of the subject and make the products of their imagining seem utterly real.

boundary perception

Any exercise that encourages people to trust strangers in an unusual environment can also switch off this boundary perception, and thus make us more susceptible to control. As our parents warned us in infancy, it is a bad idea to trust strangers automatically, so "team building" exercises – used by so many institutions – should be approached with caution.

Hypnotic or altered states can be separated into several types, which include both relaxation and euphoria. When we are relaxed or euphoric, we are more likely to be obedient and give control to a commanding outsider.[196]

Perhaps the first obvious altered state is hallucination. If attention is fixed – by staring, chanting or singing a word or phrase, marching in step or playing or dancing to the same beat – perception can change.

Meditators report seeing colored veils shifting in front of their eyes. In the traditional Hindu *tratak*, meditators stare at an object. In Scientology's "training routine zero", two people look fixedly at each other. Lurid hallucinations will occur. This is because when nothing is happening, the mind fills in the blank backdrop or amplifies the slightest signal. In the dark, we sense movement. In silence, we hear noises. This is called the Ganzfeld effect.

These are forms of *positive hallucination* – where something appears which is not there – but *negative hallucination* is also possible – where real objects vanish from perception. A hypnotized subject can become blind to any aspect of the environment, often to the amusement of onlookers.

autopilot – the default mode network

Brain imaging has revealed what is known as the default mode network, which is below awareness and might well maintain the automatic functions that we call "autopilot". When driving a car, riding a bike, or playing a musical instrument, autopilot becomes a necessity: we can't keep everything consciously in mind when performing difficult tasks.[197] We move through a variety of states both during our sleeping and waking states.

Meditation and "mindfulness" are attempts to control our state of mind. Reporting on a meta-analysis of 4,000 study reports, Dr Miguel Farias, himself a meditator and an expert on meditation, says: "Despite the anecdotal evidence on the effects of mindfulness meditation, and despite the hundreds of studies produced in the last twenty years, there was no robust scientific evidence that mindfulness has any substantial effect on our minds and behaviours."[198] Meditative states are altered states that feel good, but don't necessarily change anything but self-perception.

aspects of altered states[199]

Alterations of time are also aspects of altered states. *Age regression* is commonly used by hypnotherapists. When age regressed, people behave as if they were the age that has been suggested to them. Sometimes, they may experience real memories from an earlier age, but it is common for such subjects to create imaginary events. They are *pretending* to be a child. These false memories feel progressively more real with hour upon hour of investigation with a "past lives" counselor.

Altered states:
- positive hallucination – seeing things that aren't there
- negative hallucination – not seeing things that are there
- age regression – pretending to be a younger self
- age progression – imagining future outcomes

- amnesia – loss of memory
- hypermnesia – overly-detailed memory
- heightened perceptions

Many people believe they have found memories of past lives – this was routine when I was in Scientology: one friend insisted that he had been Judas Iscariot, and my vanity allowed me to believe that I had been Henri Matisse. There is precious little evidence for reincarnation, and in more than forty years no Scientologist has ever offered me proof of a single past life memory. It seems far more likely that such "memories" are wishful thinking. Dreams of glory are far more appealing than the daily grind, so can all too readily displace reality. We all live in our dream of the world, but the distance between the dream and reality varies greatly from one person to the next.

"Psychic" claims so often prove to be fraudulent that only with the most rigorous investigation into their veracity should they even *begin* to be believed. Between them, James Randi and Derren Brown have both managed to replicate most "psychic phenomena" from spoon-bending and remote viewing, to table-turning and poltergeist phenomena.

Age progression is just as possible as age regression. Here, people really believe that they are predicting future events. Age progression is also involved in visualization, a common practice among athletes, who believe that by imagining a positive future outcome they can create it (the practice also fires the neurons responsible for the desired action, which may well be useful).

Amnesia is another common altered state. It is easy to suggest to someone that they will forget. We have all experienced this when unable to find a word that is on the tip of the tongue. It is possible to create a state of confusion over a word, so that it will be difficult to access.

For some reason, I spent months unable to remember the Japanese word *kamikaze*, for suicide pilots. I had no difficulty in remembering the meaning of the term – spirit wind – but this somehow blocked my access to the word it defined.[200] Such amnesia is a common occurrence, in part because of the enormous demands upon memory made by everyday life in a complex civilization. We forget far more than we remember, and our memories are easily manipulated.

Opposed to hypnotic amnesia is *hyper-vigilant memory* – or hypermnesia – which must be burdensome. Some people remember accurately every day of their lives. They will often have difficulty remembering facts from their schooling, however. Different abilities and different parts of the brain are involved for episodic and factual memory.

Hypnosis allows us to retreat from the world outside into our own imaginations and even to retreat from our own bodily sensations. Hypnosis can be used to reduce the sensation of pain; many doctors and dentists use hypnosis in their practice as an analgesic. For many people, hypnosis is a completely effective painkiller.

altered perceptions

Our sensitivity to bodily sensations – including pain – changes from moment to moment. We have all found ourselves more or less sensitive to our perceptions. On some days, food has more taste, on others, it has hardly any taste at all. Heightened perception is at the opposite end of the scale to analgesia. Typically, hypnotic subjects will declare that colors are brighter, sounds are clearer, or that their bodies feel physically larger. These changes in perception overlap with hallucination, so that some subjects will even feel invisible – which is a form of negative hallucination: failing to perceive what is actually present.

The capacity to remember does not form fully until we have passed the infant stage, and even then, as we've seen, memory is replayed on the same screen as imagination. Many childhood memories have been colored both by retelling, *and* because they are family legends, often repeated. Yet, before the memory system forms properly, we have learned to interpret the world around us. Many of our conceptions about that world are formed in child-hood, before we have the capacity to interpret such conceptions properly.

It is as if we wake up in the river of consciousness years after we were thrown into it. We do not consciously form our beliefs at the earliest age. We have a simple sense of right and wrong, much of it taken from our parents and those around us. While Freud was often too confident in his assertions about the human psyche, he was probably right to assert that our relationships in life are often determined by how we attached to the caregivers of childhood.

The evidence supports the idea that those who grew up in an unsafe environment will rely on the reactive part of the brain – the old brain – and be less considered (and more aggressive or fearful) in their response to the world. In other words, they will either run away or thump you, rather than dealing with the niceties of discussion. This panicked activity is the greatest obstacle to critical thinking, because such people will also run away from evidence.

The fight-or-flight mechanism can be extended to include both "freeze" and "fawn" as other possible responses, often formed in childhood as reactions to predatory advances.

cognitive dissonance revisited

Cognitive dissonance is perhaps the most fundamental concept for an understanding of coercive control or exploitative persuasion. Every now and then, a great genius lights up the world and creates a new perspective. Leon Festinger was such a one, and his cognitive dissonance is one of the most important ideas of the last century.

Leon Festinger

New ideas take time to root and are usually ignored or opposed before they can be accepted. Darwin and Wallace's natural selection or the acceptance of an unconscious "mind" are examples of hard-fought "paradigm shifts". Indeed, "intelligent design" and notions of in-dwelling demons continue to fight a rearguard action against these well-demonstrated concepts.

Festinger's work has transformed psychology – but his name had not entered Microsoft's spell checker, more than 60 years after his profound discovery. Festinger realized that reason does not necessarily inform our decision-making. Instead, we usually hold on to our beliefs and adapt – or ignore – the facts to suit them. Any conflict between behavior, emotion and thought creates an unpleasant sensation, much like the grating dissonance between two or more inharmonious musical notes. To end this uncomfortable feeling, we will tend to reject the source – even when that source is very hard evidence indeed.

Prejudices are basic to paradigms – sets of beliefs that govern our view of the world. In Ken Burns' wonderful *Jazz* documentaries, a white aficionado explains that as a child, at the beginning of the twentieth century, in the Deep South, he was led to believe that black people were inferior to whites and incapable of intelligence. He suffered overwhelming cognitive dissonance when he first saw Louis Armstrong perform. Armstrong was quite evidently a genius. His creativity was fundamental to the development of jazz and his virtuosity transformed trumpet playing and singing in all genres of popular music.

The young white man understood that he had been fed false information, and was able to resolve the cognitive dissonance by rejecting that information. His ability to change his perspective is a lesson we should all take to heart, because *all too often we follow our beliefs instead of the evidence.*

There is no doubt that the paradigm shift that ended racial segregation in the United States was accelerated by the genius of black performers. Armstrong, Sidney Bechet, Duke Ellington, Ella Fitzgerald, Billie Holiday, Teddy Wilson, Nina Simone, Ray Charles, Nat King Cole, Harry Belafonte and a host of others showed that black people could burst with talent.

Incidentally, prejudices against Jews were challenged at the same time, through the likes of Benny Goodman, Artie Shaw and the many composers of jazz standards and musicals (most of whom were Jewish). Many of the most talented comedians and classical musicians have also been Jewish. While idiotic prejudices continue, they are no longer supported by law, as they were well into the 20th century (native Americans were not even recognized as human beings until 1924).

questioning our unquestionable assumptions

If we can be patient with our feelings of unease, and learn to question our assumptions, no matter how rigid they have become, and no matter the reverence we feel for the authority figures who taught us these assumptions, then we can transform ourselves and our society.

As prejudice is the foundation of human conflict, understanding how to resolve conflicts within ourselves, rather than on the battle-field, is probably the most important paradigm shift that we can achieve. By learning to calm our emotional responses to evidence, we can create a safer world.[201]

In recent times, we have been subjected to the War on Terror. It is always dangerous to solidify an abstract concept – to reify thoughts or emotions into concrete realities. Franklin Delano Roosevelt said that the only thing we have to fear is fear itself, but now we are fighting a war against fear, which is the very opposite of Roosevelt's dictum. We have been deftly moved from the fear of nuclear annihilation to the fear of terrorism: the fear of fear itself.[202]

This war has led to immense and irrational prejudices against Muslims. The terrorists belong to tiny factions, yet the media continues to call the few militant Wahhabis of Al-Qaeda and the Islamic State "Sunnis" (or simply "Muslims"). While the Sunnis make up the majority of Muslims, the fundamentalist Wahhabis represent perhaps one per cent, and most of these do not belong to terrorist factions. Similarly, only a fraction of Shi'ites – the other major branch of Islam – are involved in terrorist activity. But all of Islam is seen as threatening, through media manipulation or simple ignorance.

After the 7/7 bombing in London, one of my friends insisted that "Muslims" should apologize for this crime. This is like saying that Christians should apologize for the torrent of hate speech that pours out of the Westboro Baptists. However, cognitive dissonance tends towards generalization.

It is only by recognizing our frailty that we can become strong. Our unconscious processes are easily directed, and thoughts are easily led. By understanding this, we can improve our ability to learn and strengthen our defenses against the everyday manipulations of modern life.

We now turn to the most pervasive use of influence in human society: the use of propaganda, public relations and advertising.

recommended reading:

Carl Sagan, *The Demon-Haunted World*
Derren Brown, *Tricks of the Mind*.

11
life is a pitch (and then you buy)

"Our strategy ... is to destroy the enemy from within to conquer him through himself." ~ Adolf Hitler

Manipulation has become far more pervasive with the introduction of each new form of communication. Writing, printing, radio, film, television and the Internet have all extended the reach of both educators and manipulators. All manner of organizations – from the most beneficial manufacturer of essential items, to the very worst authoritarian groups – advertise their wares using every conceivable medium. By these means, influence has become institutionalized in both government and business.

Influence only becomes unethical when there is a hidden agenda and deliberate deception. There is nothing wrong with open and honest communication, but advertising is not necessarily "legal, decent, honest and truthful," to use the UK Advertising Standards Authority's definition. Authoritarian groups have no compunction about using any available method to increase their ability to recruit and retain followers.

Advertising, in the form of branding, reaches back at least to Sumeria, the cradle of civilization, where writing was first discovered. Beer bottle caps made there predate the modern crown cap by over 4000 years. This is a positive use of influence: remember our brand so that you can buy it again. By the fifth century BCE, in ancient Greece, the Sophists sold their skills of argument and oratory. Similar skills were developed at around the same time in China. In both places, these skills were also honed to create the basis of rational philosophies.

Julius Caesar was well aware of the power of imagery: he was the first ruler to put his own portrait onto coins. An authorized bust of him was distributed throughout the Roman Empire.

There is no clear dividing line between art, advertising and propaganda. For many centuries, European artists illustrated Bible stories for an illiterate population. In the Renaissance, art became a demonstration of wealth and influence, and a tool of propaganda utilized by the ruling class to maintain authority over the masses, as artists were paid to add images of their patrons to religious pictures.

In an early example of political spin, in the sixteenth century Queen Elizabeth I ordered all existing portraits of her to be destroyed. They were replaced with approved images, depicting her as a beautiful Virgin Queen. These approved images bore little resemblance to the reality.

By this time, advertising had been spurred on with the introduction of the printing press, which also heralded a new age of *propaganda* (originally the Catholic Church's term for the office that lured defectors back into the fold during the Reformation).

modern advertising

Modern advertising, however, began after the American Civil War, in the 1860s – the first modern conflict, which left a mass of physically and psychologically traumatized combatants. The pharmaceutical companies were born at this time, selling patent medicines that would be illegal today, because along with alcohol, they contained opium and cannabis. Coca leaves were added to the mix at the end of the nineteenth century, and enthusiastically endorsed by Pope Leo XIII – on billboards for Mariani wine – and by Sigmund Freud, in his early paper, *Uber Coca*. Cocaine is derived from coca leaves. Pope Leo went so far as to award a gold medal to the hard drug concoction "bearing his august effigy."[203] Many celebrated figures endorsed the wine, including Thomas Edison, Jules Verne, the Russian Empress, Emile Zola, Alexandre Dumas and Henrik Ibsen.[204] As with celebrities in contemporary advertising, it was hoped that endorsements by prominent figures would persuade the public at large that they would benefit from these products.

By the mid-twentieth century, advertising had come to include a plethora of new techniques. Corporations would now "sell the sizzle, not the steak." The housewife would be subjected to "two tarts in the kitchen" advertisements. TV medical doctor Marcus Welby, MD (actor Robert Young) sold

coffee, dressed up in a white coat. The appeal of authority gave way to the use of celebrities, so Ronald Reagan advocated not only for the Voice of America – the US anti-Communist radio station – but also Chesterfield cigarettes, in the years before his presidency.

Motivational research was exposed by Vance Packard in *The Hidden Persuaders* in 1957. The giants of industry were already apportioning millions of dollars to understand the minds of consumers.

In the 1970s, positioning theory showed that it was best to "position" your product against a market leader. Avis car rentals ran against Hertz with their "we try harder" campaign, which successfully increased their market share. In the UK, a very popular series of ads showed Leonard Rossiter spilling Cinzano on Joan Collins. Unfortunately for Cinzano, this led to a

surge in market leader Martini's sales. The outcome of covert influence is not always predictable.

Next came aspirational "lifestyle" marketing, where the product was seen as part of an envied lifestyle. Sharper Image exemplifies this approach, where the customer buys in to a way of life rather than a product. As Erich Fromm argued, it is possible that the majority of people rely upon approval from others, rather than developing their own individuality.[205] He would call such people "benign narcissists".[206]

Focus groups are employed throughout the public relations trade, to pinpoint the public's wants and vulnerabilities. For instance, after their slump in popularity after rushing into the second Iraq war, the UK New Labour party quizzed their "floating voter" focus groups to see what measure might win them the next election. These floating voters were mainly housewives in their thirties. It transpired that they were most annoyed about neighbors who left their garbage bins on the sidewalk (or pavement), so a law was quickly enacted to restrict the time of day that bins were permitted on the sidewalk. No UK council has ever enforced this law, but New Labour won another term, at least in part because of pandering to the taste of those who were politically undecided.

Advertisers can afford the latest in technology, so by the 1990s, CT scanners were being used for "neuromarketing" surveys. Instead of relying on verbal answers to questions – which might be influenced by the desire to please the questioner – volunteers were brain-scanned to see what their real uncensored responses were.

Coca-Cola was among the first corporations to use this new technique. This led to "emotional" marketing, which tries to tap straight into the emotional centers of the brain. The most profound allegiances are rerouted, so, for instance, one fan of Pepsi talked about the patriotic rush he felt when looking at the red, white and blue logo on the can.

These days, manufacturers contribute to the funding for movies, with the guarantee that their products will feature prominently in the resulting film. This "product placement" may very well work at a hypnotic level.

The whole drift of advertising is to induce an experience, to create an emotional demand for a product or service. And advertising is a mainstay of modern life. We watch films and go to concerts, because we want to be *given* an experience. Sitting at home and watching a film on the TV, or listening to music on a home sound system, is quite different from participating in a group. This receptivity to group experience makes us more susceptible to the contrived tricks of exploiters. We experience a natural high when in company, whether it is a rock concert or a political rally. That innocent high is easily manipulated.

public relations and propaganda

The grip of the Catholic Church was significantly weakened when the Bible was translated into everyday language, and the public discovered there were no priests, no monks, and no mention of buying a stairway to heaven through "indulgences" in the Good Book. William Tyndale, whose translation formed the basis of one of the greatest literary works in English, the King James Bible, was burned at the stake for the "heresy" of making the Bible available to non-Latin speakers.

Protestant propagandists soon created lurid tales of the Catholic Inquisition, although more innocents actually died at the hands of their own witch hunters. These exaggerations are believed to this day along with many other propaganda myths.[207] The fervor with which such dogma was believed during the wars of the Reformation and the witch hunts fits the same template as the fanaticism of contemporary authoritarian groups.

1879 was a turning point in human history: the new photogravure process allowed photographs to be printed on ordinary paper, allowing Progressive journalists to show the world at large the horrors of poverty and child labor. Called "muckrakers" by President Teddy Roosevelt, the Progressives refined techniques that would soon be adopted by less ethical persuaders.

At the opening of the twentieth century, public relations became big business, after Edward Bernays asked his uncle, Sigmund Freud, how to influence people by appealing directly to their sexual urge. Freud was happy to oblige. There is certainly evidence to support our attraction to sexually stimulating images and sounds (and should human pheromones eventually be tracked down, probably to scents). Bernays believed that success in advertising derived from subliminal persuasion, and he applied that information from the birth of modern PR – or *propaganda* as he called it – through the many decades of his unusually long life.

Bernays represented Lucky Strike cigarettes for many years. The original cigarette pack was drab green

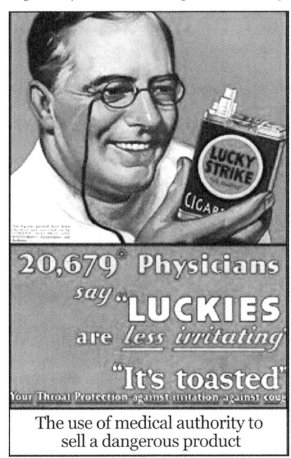

20,679* Physicians say "LUCKIES are *less irritating*"

"It's toasted"

Your Throat Protection against irritation against cough

The use of medical authority to sell a dangerous product

with a red circle. Bernays decided to make a connection between the brand and the proto-feminist movement of the 1930s. He had women dressed in Lucky Strike colors, parading around while proudly smoking the brand –which Bernays called "torches of freedom" – in a time when it was considered *vulgar* for a woman to smoke in public. It was a statement of defiance, a great propaganda stunt and stealth influence rolled into one. As both the tobacco company and the women's rights group were clients, the shrewd Bernays was even paid twice.[208]

Bernays' many successful campaigns led to ever more influence: for instance, he handled the PR end of the overthrow of the democratic Guatemalan government for United Fruit (and the Eisenhower administration). He was party to Vice-President Richard Nixon's much-publicized visit to congratulate the newly appointed puppet dictator, in 1954.

controlling the masses

Bernays agreed with theorist Walter Lippmann that it was necessary for the élite to control the masses through public relations, until such time as the masses were educated enough to create a real democracy. This insidious perspective, which continues to this day among patrician capitalists, is identical with the elitist views of authoritarian groups. We tend to see *public relations* as relatively positive and *propaganda* as absolutely negative. And yet, until his death at the age of 103, Bernays insisted that *propaganda* and *public relations* are one and the same.

Also starting at the beginning of the twentieth century, Ivy Lee made his name as one of the first modern propagandists, using techniques focusing on emotional manipulation, rather than reasoning. He is famous for his part in protecting Exxon – as it is more recently known – from the bad public relations resulting from the murder of trade unionists. For instance, Lee characterized activist Mother Jones as a "bawdy prostitute." She was, in fact, almost 80 years old by this time and had lived an exemplary life fighting for the rights of the under-privileged.

World War One saw the amalgamation of public relations and progressive journalism in the US Committee on Public Information. The Bureau of Cartoons (!) sent out the *Weekly Bulletin for Cartoonists* to 750 cartoonists, with ideas and captions for the coming week's fare. The Division of Films courted Hollywood.

Film is the perfect medium for propaganda and has tremendous potential to manipulate an audience's beliefs. Foreign film distributors were forced to show Allied war pictures alongside their features, and cinemas that showed German films were simply denied any new Hollywood material.

In American cities, 75,000 Four-Minute Men, pillars of their communities, stood up twice a week and burst into apparently spontaneous speeches at cinemas or other public places. Their impassioned "impromptu" talks were based on bulletins dispatched by the Committee on Public Information (CPI). They defended capitalism, attacked "Prussianism" and used President Wilson's tag line, often heard since, "Make the world safe for democracy!"

The CPI wanted to provide both the material and the sentiment for everyday conversation. Dissent would be quelled, and the proper patriotic attitude maintained. The Four-Minute Men also sold war bonds. One CPI bulletin advised "One idea – simple language – talk in pictures, not in statistics – touch their minds, hearts, spirits – make them want to win with every fiber of their beings – translate that desire into terms of bonds – and they will buy."

Within a short period of time, the Committee on Public Information had outposts in 30 countries, which daily poured forth pro-Allied and anti-Axis sentiments. The CPI picked up techniques that had earlier been used to neutralize antagonism between labor and management. It was also economical with the truth, suppressing unfavorable information and censoring dangerous ideas. This was the beginning of our contemporary age of spin.

Congress passed the Espionage Act, upholding censorship, and later the Sedition Act, which made it illegal to criticize the government. Many American citizens were arrested without charge and imprisoned without bail, losing any access to the outside world. One adolescent girl was sentenced to 20 years in prison for her protest.[209]

With the end of the First World War, the Committee on Public Information disbanded, but its journalists, advertising agents and propagandists stayed in touch. With the Second War, the same cast of characters assembled, and, beyond that war, created a network that ran media outlets, advertising and PR agencies as well as government intelligence agencies. It was deemed necessary by those in power in the West to utilize war-time methods to prevent communism from taking over the world. Similar justifications are now used to support ever more vigorous control of communication by government agencies.

media as mind control

Nazi Germany was the first state to achieve control using mass media. At his trial, Albert Speer, Hitler's minister for armaments, said, "Hitler's dictatorship differed in one fundamental from all its predecessors in history. It was the first dictatorship in the present period of modern development, a dictatorship which made complete use of all technical means for the domination of its own country. *"Through technical devices like the radio and the loud-speaker, eighty million people were deprived of independent thought. It was thereby possible to subject them to the will of one man."*

We hear of the great firewall of China these days. News reports show that the Chinese government still encourages the population to spy on one another – just as agents of the Gestapo did under Hitler. It is alleged that credit reports in China are now linked to social media: if you criticize the state, your credit rating will collapse. Facial recognition systems have been linked to surveillance cameras in some provinces. China has also artfully managed to restrict information about the continued use of "brainwashing" camps. In 2018, news broke that over a million people – largely Uighur Muslims – were being "re-educated" in these camps.

After the Second World War, Western governments poured funds into covert programs to determine the laws of behavior and so control people without their knowledge or consent. Allied governments wanted to know how to incapacitate enemy soldiers, so they introduced LSD to students, accidentally kick-starting the hippie movement. They used the far more savage drug, BZ, on hundreds of unwitting American GIs. BZ gives flashbacks lasting for days, which can recur for life. It is now restricted under the Chemical Weapons Convention.

The president of the World Federation of Mental Health used his Canadian hospital to experiment on unwitting patients who were given to believe that they were receiving treatment for illness. Sensory deprivation and electric shocks were used to completely erase the memories of patients suffering from depression. The attempt to create a programable zombie – a Manchurian candidate – failed, because whilst it proved relatively easy to destroy memory, rebuilding it proved to be impossible.[210]

As we've seen, the Unification Church – the Moonies – came into being after its creator, Sun Myung Moon, used "brainwashing" techniques in the Victory Over Communism program, in South Korea. He had been subjected to these techniques in a North Korean prison. The rapid growth of Daesh or the Islamic State has been driven by the determined use of coercive control in propaganda across social media. As we have seen, the techniques they are using were developed by western propagandists.

We need to be aware of the whole array of methods available to manipulators, whether they are leaders of authoritarian groups, corporate advertisers, or governments eager to manipulate the beliefs of the electorate.

Naomi Klein has offered a cogent argument that such techniques – and the inhumane attitudes behind them – have been employed as significant elements in the War on Terror.[211] At Guantanamo Bay, and in "extraordinary rendition" torture sites around the world, the US military put into practice the methods used in the post-Second War mind control projects. This secret manipulation is our inheritance.

In the next chapter, we will consider the case of Louise Ogborn, a shocking real-life example of coercive control.

recommended reading:

Pratkanis and Aranson, *Age of Propaganda: The Everyday Use and Abuse of Persuasion*
Stuart Ewen, *PR! A Social History of Spin.*

12

coercive control:
the science and the law

"A substantial proportion of people do what they are told to do, irrespective of the content of the act, and without pangs of conscience, so long as they perceive that the command comes from a legitimate authority." ~ Stanley Milgram

Louise Ogborn was an 18-year-old high school graduate when she took a job at a McDonald's in Mount Washington, Kentucky, to help her mother, who had lost her job. Louise wanted to study pre-med at college, but the trauma of events at the restaurant wrecked her plans. Ogborn was a church-going former Girl Scout, and had not received a single admonition in the four months that she had worked at the restaurant.

It was just after 5 pm when assistant manager Donna Jean Summers took a call from "Officer Scott", who said he was with the local police. "Scott" told her that an employee had been accused of stealing a purse. From his broad description, Summers identified Ogborn as the culprit. Scott asked Summers to search Ogborn, otherwise, she would be arrested and searched at the police station.

Ogborn was ushered into a back room and ordered to remove her clothes, while Scott stayed on the phone. Summers then followed Scott's directions to put the clothes in her own car, leaving Ogborn with only a dirty apron to cover herself. By this time, Officer Scott had told Summers that Ogborn's house was being searched for drugs.

Officer Scott next persuaded the assistant manager to summon her fiancé and to leave the young woman in his charge. The fiancé, Walter Wes Nix, Jr., followed Officer Scott's instructions, and ordered Louise Ogborn to perform jumping jacks and stand naked on a chair, while he inspected her, to ensure that she had not secreted anything inside her body.

If Ogborn refused to follow an order, at Officer Scott's direction, Nix slapped her naked buttocks until she complied. She was left prey to Scott's orders for two hours. During this time, she was ordered to sit on Nix's lap and kiss him. Then she was ordered to unzip Nix's trousers, despite all of her pleas. Nix was later sentenced to five years imprisonment for his actions.

Police estimate that "Officer Scott" was successful in manipulating staff in at least 74 workplaces, over a period of almost ten years. While staff at several of those restaurants have been convicted of offences, the man identified as "Officer Scott" by police was eventually acquitted. Louise Ogborn was paid $1.1 million in settlement by McDonald's.

Louise Ogborn explained: "My parents taught me when an adult tells you to do something, you don't argue. If someone swipes you on the hand, you listen."[212] Her ordeal was filmed by security cameras and made its way onto YouTube.[213] Police investigations showed that "Officer Scott" had tried ten other restaurants that day, but even this one in eleven success rate is startling.

Louise Ogborn's ordeal lasted for two and a half hours. When Nix left the restaurant, Summers called in maintenance man Thomas Simms, and asked him to take over. Simms, a ninth-grade drop-out, point blank refused. Summers finally called her manager and stopped the assault. She was later convicted of unlawful imprisonment and sentenced to a year's probation. Summers was paid $400,000 in settlement by McDonald's.

It is horrifying to note that the man identified by police as "Officer Scott" was acquitted for lack of evidence, and because it is so hard to define his actual crime. It is interesting that the first person to stand up to Officer Scott's orders was the least educated in academic terms. *The upshot is that we teach our children to be cautious of strangers, but not simply of **strangeness***.

We should withdraw and seek better information before complying with any request that seems in the least bizarre.

When an unusual demand is made, it should prompt questioning and resistance rather than compliance. As Ira Chaleff shows in his fine book, *Intelligent Disobedience*, such training is lacking in our educational system or even as a principle instilled by parents. Chaleff also exposes the training given to schoolteachers that imposes obedience on students using highly questionable techniques.

Bertrand Russell warned, "It is to be expected that advances in psychology will give governments much more control over individual mentality than they have now ... *Education should aim at destroying free will, so that, after pupils have left school, they shall be incapable, throughout the rest of their lives, of thinking or acting otherwise than as their schoolmaster would have wished.*"[214] This is certainly far from the intent of all decent teachers, but schools continue to prepare their pupils to act obediently, just as poor Louise Ogborn did.

Although she put up some resistance, in the end, and out of fear, Louise Ogborn capitulated to the terrible demands of Officer Scott. Her compliance is understandable; it is far harder to understand the compliant behavior of any of the other participants and spectators, who did nothing to stop these events.

The story seems far-fetched, but there are more than 70 cases where a caller successfully targeted restaurants or grocery stores in the US, and convinced managers to strip search and, at times, participate in the sexual abuse of store workers. The movie *Compliance* and the short film *Plainview* are both based upon "Officer Scott's" despicable hoax calls. They illustrate the need to transform our relationship to authority.

Those of us who have helped former members of authoritarian groups find it hard to understand the reluctance of some social scientists to accept the reality of manipulation, exploitative persuasion, thought reform or coercive control. The point is regularly made that members join of their own free will and that nothing compels them to remain within the confines of an authoritarian group. But the point is made as if such a belief is factual and natural, and beyond any slightest shadow of doubt. Science always allows room for doubt just as authoritarian beliefs never can.

the long history of coercive control

In truth, coercive control was recognized in law centuries before the term "social science" was first heard. For more than 500 years, "undue influence" has been a legitimate legal concept to provide remedy for the victims of swindlers. The law of undue influence was framed because of concerns that exploitative churchmen were taking advantage of the deathbed fears of the faithful.[215]

In 1617, a woman who rejoiced in the name of Mrs. Death made something of a media splash, when the eminent jurist and philosopher Lord

Francis Bacon tried her case. The following comes from Lord Bacon's ruling, and speaks of Mrs. Death's hapless victim, Mr. Lydiatt:

"An old man about the age of eighty years and being weak of body and understanding and having a great estate of goods and lands ... was drawn by the practices and indirect means ... to give his house here in London and to come to sojourn with her [and her husband, Mr. Death] at her house in the country ... and that she having him there did so work upon his simplicity and weakness and by her dalliance and pretense of love unto him and of intention after the death of her then husband to marry him, and by sundry adulterous courses with him and by sorcery and by drawing of his affections from ... his kindred, telling him sometimes that they would poison him and sometimes that they would rob him."

Sorcery, indeed. A later commentator takes up the tale:

"After she had obtained control of his estate and property, Mrs. Death neglected such attendance of him as she had used before and used him in a most cruel manner reviling him and causing him to be whipped and suffered him to lie loathsomely and uncleanly in bed until three o'clock in the afternoon without anybody to help him so as all the skin of his loins went off, he being not able to help himself by reason he was troubled with a dead palsy and other diseases, and when at any time she did come to help him up she would pinch him and revile him and by such cruel and terrible courses kept him so in awe as that he durst not revoke what before he had done, neither would she suffer his nieces to come unto him lest he should make his moan unto them, for she said if they came there she would scald them out of her house."[216]

Lord Bacon determined that Mrs. Death had no right to the property of poor Mr. Lydiatt. He had left his property to her when subjected to "undue influence." Since that time, hundreds of cases of undue influence have been heard around the world, yet some social scientists believe that undue influence is a new and unwelcome concept that can be dismissed with a shrug as "brainwashing". They are wrong.

It has been accepted for centuries that anyone in authority has a special position. There is a *presumption* of undue influence. So, if you give a car, a house or even a box of chocolates to your lawyer, to your priest or to your counselor, you can claim it back. You don't have to prove anything, and this law puts aside any need for guilt to be demonstrated. If you gave it away, you can claim it back, because of *presumed undue influence*.

In Mrs. Death's case, the influence went beyond *presumption*. She was charged with "express" or "active" undue influence, for her use of the lock and the rod, and for the dismal conditions that Mr. Lydiatt had suffered at her hands. She did not inherit a single penny.

recognizing undue influence

The nature of manipulation was also recognized by the Nuremburg War Crimes Tribunal. Nazis born after 1919, save for those who had committed the most heinous crimes, were exempted from prosecution, because they had been indoctrinated throughout childhood into the aberrant and abhorrent beliefs of National Socialism.[217]

In his excellent article on undue influence, Abraham Nieven, PhD, cites the California Civil Code Section 1575:

In the use, by one in whom a confidence is reposed by another, or who holds a real or apparent authority over him, of such confidence or authority for the purpose of obtaining an unfair advantage over him;

In taking an unfair advantage of another's weakness of mind; or

In taking a grossly oppressive and unfair advantage of another's necessities or distress.[218]

Members of authoritarian groups often work a ninety-hour week for only a few dollars in pay. I have interviewed literally hundreds who at one time or another were reduced to a diet of rice and beans, often for months at a time, while their boss chowed down on *pâté de foie gras* and quenched his thirst with blue mountain coffee made with purified water.

Yet, there is no legal protection for those in these authoritarian relationships, unless they realize that they have been subjected to undue influence (or "coercive control"). By the time they do, they will have left the relationship and be too taken up with recovery to even consider bringing undue influence charges for the return of monies squeezed out of them, or fair recompense for their labor. They will also tend to be terrified of the authoritarian, and by the time they recover, the statute of limitations – the time allowed for litigation – may well have passed.

It has long been recognized that selling techniques can break down resistance, and that even rational, intelligent people can succumb to a hard sell. In the UK, we have a legal "cooling off" period of seven days after signing a contract.

Social scientists who reject the idea of undue influence or coercive control are the newcomers in this time-honored field. They are also in the minority:

most of us recognize that we have at times been tricked into buying some useless artifact because of a sales pitch. The ego is unwilling to accept this, because the illusion of free will is so complete, so such personal errors are downplayed.[219] Because social scientists have not presented the true and harrowing reality of undue influence, governments have failed to act. There is no protection whatsoever for those who have given everything they owned (and often everything they could borrow) to an abusive authoritarian group.

Emeritus professor of law Alan Scheflin has spent a lifetime studying undue influence. He is well-known as the co-author of *The Mind Manipulators*, which details the mind control experiments of US intelligence agencies.[220] In 2014, Scheflin produced the fruits of decades of study, the Social Influence Model.[221] The model provides a framework to estimate the degree of influence, and therefore the relative responsibility of those accused of criminal acts or civil torts. Scheflin has worked for decades in the attempt to reform the judicial system with regard to undue or predatory influence. As the law accepts undue influence, it is strange that the judicial system resists rational change to accept its consequences in all areas of life. Scheflin's social influence model is given as an appendix to this book.[222]

Now we turn to the evidence for coercive control.

recommended reading:

Compliance, director Craig Zobel, 2012
Scheflin, Alan, "Supporting Human Rights by Testifying Against Human Wrongs" Paul Martin Lecture, 2014

13
the evidence for coercive control

"Man is made by belief. As he believes, so he is." ~Bhagavad Gita

To resist coercive control, we have to accept that it is a proven reality, not the figment of the imagination suggested by a few resolute social scientists. The first experimental proof of an "unconscious mind" came relatively late – in 1977 – but once it became clear that some part of thinking takes place beneath consciousness, it was also clear that influence – and thusly coercive control – can and must occur.

Anyone who doubts the existence of influence should watch a few Derren Brown shows. For the sake of entertainment and illumination, Derren Brown has cast a wide net in search of scams both old and new. He has revisited the tricks of the 19th century Spiritualists, and shown how innocents can be persuaded to turn tables, make bells ring and write on "sealed" tablets, all the while believing these actions were impelled by some outer force.

Brown is an accomplished hypnotist, and in a matter of moments can install a false memory in what appears to be an innocent conversation. In one show, a fifteen-minute exchange was all it took to convince a lifelong atheist of the presence of God – without any theological discussion.[223] In another, four business executives each individually held up a security van at gunpoint, before being brought out of trance.[224]

Brown also took on the famed objective of the US intelligence agencies, the Manchurian Candidate, a programmable assassin. The CIA had pronounced it impossible (perhaps untruthfully), but Brown's subject fired a gun at actor Stephen Fry, without knowing that it contained blanks.[225] His

2016 *Pushed to the Edge* (also known as *The Push*) showed just how quickly and easily people can be persuaded to murder another person for the good of a cause. *It took just a few hours and nothing more than the dynamics of human compliance to bring relatively ordinary people to kill a man, believing they were saving a charitable cause by doing so.*

proof versus conviction

Galileo had trouble with the astronomers who refused to look through his telescope, insisting that he first prove that the Medici stars, the moons orbiting Jupiter, *could* exist, given the accepted presence of the crystal spheres, on which the sun and planets revolve around the earth.[226] This same perplexity faces the counselor who helps former members gather their wits after departing an authoritarian relationship, when faced with those sociologists who believe that such relationships are freely entered into and freely maintained.

The notion that coercive control does not exist also stretches the boundaries of credibility when we look at the most deplorable mysteries of human behavior. How could Stalin, Hitler and Mao run concentration camps where so many millions died?[227] How did Pol Pot manage to destroy a quarter of the Cambodian population in a few short years, and why did the world stand by, apparently indifferent?

authority and obedience

The dynamics of coercive control exist in every human society and, indeed, in every human being. We are all subject to groupthink, to following the herd, to believing ideas without proper consideration, and to offering our obedience, because we *all* too easily accept the authority of those who spout those ideas. As Scientology's creator Ron Hubbard said, all authority relationships are hypnotic: "Any time anybody gets enough altitude he can be called a hypnotic operator, and what he says *will* act as hypnotic suggestion."[228]

Oscar Wilde expressed the simplest answer when he said: *"disobedience is Man's original virtue."* Our ability to question even the toughest groupthink is vital.

After studying a dozen contemporary authoritarian groups in some detail, and taking a long look at the history of religion, from the *Mystes* of Ancient Greece up to the present day, I turned my attention to political and social movements, including the Nazis and the Bolsheviks. From there I studied gangs and terrorist groups. The dynamics of all authoritarian groups are remarkably similar, simply because human psychology doesn't change from one group to another.

There is a continuum of authoritarianism, from the abusive partner to the totalist state. The power of choice is taken away in these relationships: they are undemocratic and tyrannical in nature. As a species, we need to evolve away from authoritarianism in all of our relationships and all of our institutions.

My own departure from Scientology was spurred by historian Norman Cohn's fine *Pursuit of the Millennium,* which I read two years before I resigned from the group. Cohn was writing about movements between 1000 and 1250 CE, whose followers fervently believed in the imminent Second Coming of Jesus, and murdered Jews, Muslims and fellow Christians in their thirst to bring about the End Days.

Shortly before I read Cohn, Hubbard had warned that World War III was imminent, so this fascinating book planted the seeds of doubt in me. I was witnessing irrational behavior in my fellow Scientologists which was frighteningly similar to that described by Cohn in the fanatics who destroyed all around them, through their conviction that the end of the world was very nigh indeed. I went on to Cohn's *Europe's Inner Demons,* about the murderous witch craze, and found it no more reassuring.

As a believer, I cheerfully read books criticizing Scientology, but no one else I knew did the same. Criticisms were simply batted away, and the focus shifted to the critic, who would be pilloried *ad hominem.* This emotive response bothered me. Why couldn't we just examine and check the evidence and talk it through? I still believed in Scientology, but it had become irrefutable: I was involved in a fanatical group. *Any group that is unwilling to consider evidence about itself has become fanatical.*

Sixteen years after I left Scientology, with the new millennium just around the corner, I was fascinated by an interview with Norman Cohn, who, now aged more than 90, had returned to public view to warn of incipient millenarianism. He proved to be right, but thankfully not on the feared scale – in Uganda, for instance, 778 members of the Movement for the Restoration of the Ten Commandments of God immolated themselves, assured by their leader of the end of the world.[229]

In the interview, Cohn explained that, at the end of World War Two, he had worked in the denazification unit, alongside Russian officers.[230] He said that it was apparent to him that the Soviets suffered from the same irrational and driven fanaticism as the Nazis. He readily described them as "cult members."

terrorism

Reading about terrorists in the early 1990s, it became obvious that the dynamics of coercive control and fanaticism exist wherever we look. Everywhere in the world, people respond to the same sort of pressures with their own local variations. The dynamics within a terrorist cell or a gang are found in other authoritarian relationships and destructive groups. I was surprised that learned authorities scorned what they mistakenly called "brainwashing", even castigating my expert friends by name. They offered up "radicalization" instead, but without giving any explanation of this process, beyond such ideas as the "bunch of guys hypothesis",[231] which insists that Muslim lads get together to play soccer for a lark and the next thing you know, after a quick pizza, they are strapping on suicide belts. Who knew that soccer and pizza could be so dangerous?

While the work of such experts as Sageman, Post and Atran is full of fascinating information, it stops short of any useful explanation. For all the light they shine on radicalization, they might just as well have stuck with the tabloid term "brainwashing."

Could it be that the behavior recorded by Robert Jay Lifton in interviews with survivors of the Chinese thought-reform camps not only applied to authoritarian groups, but also to terrorist cells? Were these universal human weaknesses that might be exploited by the vicious and the manipulative?

The essential understanding is that *the dynamics of human behavior are always and everywhere broadly the same.* Confirmation or "myside" bias operates in all cultures: we pay more attention to evidence that supports our prejudices than we do to anything disconfirming and therefore disconcerting. This is the nature of the cognitive dissonance that any disagreement with our values entails. The Rajneeshee who is unwilling to even consider evidence that their founder was a trickster, despite the many contradictions in his work and life, is in this way no different from the fervent Maoist or the terrorist, because their fervor is an aspect of the human condition. Their powers of reasoning have been overwhelmed by their emotions.

mind control

There is a significant literature on coercive control, largely because the US military poured funding into research after World War Two. Professor Christopher Simpson found that over 90% of psychological research in the

US in the two decades after the war was sponsored by the military: "Military, intelligence, and propaganda agencies such as the Department of Defense and Central Intelligence Agency helped to bankroll substantially all of the post-World War II generation's research into techniques of persuasion, opinion measurement, interrogation, political and military mobilization, propagation of ideology, and related questions. The persuasion studies, in particular, provided much of the scientific underpinning for modern advertising and motivational techniques. This government-financed communication research went well beyond what would have been possible with private sector money alone and often exploited military recruits, who comprised a unique pool of test subjects."[232]

Alongside the top secret and life-destroying MK Ultra, MK Naomi and Operation Blue Bird programs, we also owe some of the excellent research conducted by professors Stanley Milgram and Philip Zimbardo to this funding.

One of the most researched and most significant explorations was Leon Festinger's work on cognitive dissonance. It is more than 60 years since Festinger first proposed the notion that disconfirming evidence usually hardens belief, contrary to common sense. As we have seen, when he infiltrated graduate students into a Scientology-related flying saucer cult, Festinger accurately predicted that those members who travelled to the pick-up point would leave with an even firmer faith when the mothership failed to show.[233]

We face the same difficulty in persuading entrenched social scientists of the abundant evidence that manipulation does take place, and that coercive control is a reality. And beyond the social scientists come unscientifically-minded politicians into whose hands we place the fate of the world. We have to overcome their cognitive dissonance, and persuade them to listen to reason and follow evidence rather than belief.

In a culture that is permeated with spin and artifice, there is great reluctance to accept straightforward truth. Our political culture of spin is at just as much risk as authoritarian cult groups, should the facts about coercive control become commonly known.

We have become cynical, already knowing all too well that those in power always keep an eye on their popularity, quite willing to pounce on irrelevant but emotionally upsetting issues to enlist our support. The failure of politicians as a class has been evidenced by the support for Donald Trump as the Republican presidential candidate and by the Brexit vote for the UK to leave the European Economic Community.[234]

In France, Emmanuel
Macron was able to form
a new political party and
take 60% of the National
Assembly as well as the
presidency against the
traditional parties within
a year of forming a new
party. We are sick of politicians, which is a shame,
as most of them are prob-
ably decent, well-meaning
people. They have made
the mistake of allowing
image-makers to make
them look like tricksters.

With massive unem-
ployment, there will al-
ways be a loud focus on
scroungers, who actually

have an insignificant effect on the larger economy, but can be used as a target
for ire, to unite the public behind any raging politico. Hitler spoke about the
need to attack an enemy to bring about unity among followers.

Politicians rarely demur from exploiting this vulnerability to their own
ends. Leaders of authoritarian groups are well aware that a common enemy
creates greater unity among believers.

the paradox of undue influence

The great problem with coercive control or undue influence is that it has
a *before* and an *after*, but no *during*. While individuals are under the coercive
influence, they will swear blind that they are acting out of their own free
will. They *choose* to be overworked, undernourished and frantic, to accept
the domineering alpha behavior of their overlords (or overladies). The moment the veil lifts – which can take decades – they are usually without the
strength to do anything but crawl away and weep, covered in wounds which
need a great deal of licking.

The vision of the embittered "apostate" currently trumpeted by Scientology and Jehovah's Witness mouthpieces is a falsehood; fully 99% of leavers do not protest, because they are terrified of being subjected to the "fair game policy", where they can be sued, harassed, cheated, deceived, and, as Hubbard openly said, "destroyed" or "ruined utterly" without their persecutor being restrained by the group.[235] They are not embittered so much as terrified.

Authoritarian groups with religious pretensions, like the Jehovah's Witnesses, will threaten the member's eternity. Many leave Scientology with the terror of "losing their immortality" – the belief that they will fall into the "abyss" and be lost forever. With this paralyzing phobia, the member's fate is sealed.

I once spoke to a man who was housebound for 20 years, because Scientology had convinced him that he was a danger to society. It took only an afternoon to help him back to life. If only someone had helped him 20 years earlier! To suggest that he "chose" to exclude himself from life is an insult to him and to human nature. He was a very likeable man, who would not have harmed a fly, so Scientology's persuasion was entirely misplaced.

Capricious rules can be very dangerous indeed, such as the Jehovah's Witnesses shifting sanctions about transfusions, leading thousands of members to give up their lives rather than accepting blood.

Attempts to force intervention on authoritarian group members through the law have too often run aground. There is a danger and a difficulty in presuming the individual incapable of decision, especially when we are speaking of coercive control, rather than insanity.

The US courts convicted Charles Manson of multiple murders, although he was only present at one of those murders. He was held to have manipulated his followers into committing these horrific crimes, but they too were sentenced, as if his manipulation was *not* the reason for their terrible behavior. This shows our unwillingness to accept a totality of in-

Charles Manson, leader of the infamous "Family"

fluence, and, in this circumstance, it was probably the most sensible position to take.[236] Manson's direction mitigated the murderous behavior he seems to have induced, but it does not excuse it.

But while we should all be held accountable for our behavior, no matter how drunk, drugged or deluded, those who deliberately manipulate others should also be held to account. If this means that certain practices have to be suspended in the training of monastic novices or rookie soldiers, then so be it, but the most important aspect of coercive control is probably its esoteric nature, and we can do something about that. We can make the tricks public, so that every schoolchild will recognize them on sight, and dismiss the manipulator as a fraud.

only education can overcome coercive control

As long as influential social scientists disagree with the traditional perspective of undue influence, no progress can be made in teaching schoolchildren how to recognize and overcome that influence. How sensible it would be to teach all children the pitfalls of cognitive dissonance, and about our susceptibility to Stockholm syndrome and *learned helplessness*. However, the political will is lacking, because our system too often turns politicians into vote-collecting tricksters, ignorant of science and unwilling to tackle popular taboos, in case they lose their authority and so their power.

We live in a confusing world: while one faction of social scientists decries coercive control in the universities, another faction takes its pay from the politicians, to use those same techniques as high-salaried spin doctors.

The essential aspect of reform is educational. If we want to reduce the number of terrorists, we must seek fairness for the populations they believe they represent, and also provide a general education in the techniques common to advertising, marketing, sales and recruitment. Only if people are aware of these techniques will they lose their potency. What is more, we have the task of spreading that awareness in a world long governed by spin.

Unfortunately, as we shall see, our educational system is riddled with coercive control, and professionals are too late spotting the signs in an at-risk family.

recommended reading/viewing:

Opton and Scheflin, *The Mind Manipulators.*
Roger Nygard's film *Suckers*, which reveals car dealers' tricks.

14

from domestic abuse
to college hazing

"Our key finding is that the domestic violence revolution appears to have had little effect on coercive control, the most widespread and devastating strategy men use to dominate women in personal life. Refocusing research, advocacy, law, policy, and institutional services on coercive control would be a giant step toward changing this situation." ~ Evan Stark.[237]

My work has mainly involved authoritarian groups, but I long ago noticed the similarities between them and criminal gangs and terrorist groups. This is not really surprising, as all groups share the common dynamics of human behavior, both positive and negative. We've applied Lifton's criteria for thought reform to a radicalized suicide bomber, and seen our natural tendency to submit; the same criteria are also highly relevant to intimate relationships and families.

Margaret Singer was among the first psychologists to point out that many women are *imprisoned* in intimate relationships. Her work with "brainwashed" GIs returning from Korea revealed many traits in common between abused spouses and prisoners of war. People can be trapped in a coercive relationship just as securely as they can be trapped in a prison camp. And, of course, hostages often develop a strong emotional bond with their captors.

In 1973, robbers held bank staff hostage for six days in Stockholm. Although two police officers were shot, and captor Jan-Erik Olsson threatened to kill hostages, the four hostages nonetheless defended their captors and said that they had been more frightened of the police. One of the hostages later befriended a captor after his release from prison. The incident gave the term *Stockholm Syndrome* to the world.

Learned helplessness was discovered accidentally by psychologist Martin Seligman. His team was measuring responses in dogs that were harnessed. One day, they forgot to put the harnesses on, and found that the dogs did nothing to evade the punishment that was part of the experiment.[238]

People who have been repeatedly abused often come to accept the abuse. Victims of domestic violence are often blamed for not leaving the abuser, but life isn't that simple. Apart from financial realities making it prohibitively expensive for many people to leave an established household, we can become emotionally attached to destructive people, and good-hearted, well-meaning individuals tend to forgive and try to find the best in their partner. With criticism comes low self-esteem, too, so the abused person will begin to believe the criticism. Isolation from the world separates the abused person from a more realistic estimation of their worth.

Recent thinking suggests that the focus on domestic *violence* has failed those in abusive relationships, because the violence is an expression of coercive control, and the effects of this control are even more devastating than physical violence.

In the UK, the 2015 Serious Crime Act recognized this danger and outlawed "Controlling or coercive behavior in an intimate or family relationship". Offenders can be sentenced to as much as five years in prison for inflicting *psychological* damage.

An authoritarian spouse will reduce a partner to subservience. Their behavior is narcissistic, without the slightest concern for anyone but themselves. At worst, this leads to murder.

In 1983, Diane Downs shot her three children, killing one of them. She continues to claim that she had nothing to do with the crime and was a victim. This is

Diane Downs

consistent with the psychopathic disorder – psychopaths feel no responsibility for their own actions, nor any remorse for their victims' pain.

the story of Kelsey Anne

Coercive control does not necessarily lead to violence. In the case of a young woman who identifies herself only as "Kelsey Anne", her partner never hit her, not even once. However, she was afraid – afraid of having male friends, of even talking to male co-workers. "You can do it," he would say, if she asked him for permission to go out or do anything else independently. "Just remember that every action has consequences." After a while, she simply stopped asking and stayed at home.

She had to give up her closest male friend; even female friends were not encouraged. Even though the finances were in her name, because his credit was bad, he brought her to believe that she couldn't afford to be without him. At first, she felt bombarded by his love: he flew halfway across the world to Africa just to be with her for her birthday, but he did not allow her to go to Mexico with her girlfriends.

Double standards abounded – they were both full-time students and she somehow managed a full-time job, but she did all their coursework, and he expected her to cook and clean as well. When tempers grew heated, he raised his voice, but she was not allowed to "speak to him like that."

Rather than comfort her during bouts of depression, he blamed her for "not being strong enough" and "victimizing herself." Her family and the few close friends she retained did not like him; he demanded she limit contact with them. He kept her confused with shifting emotions; one moment, she was "just a bitch," the next, he was declaring his undying love, telling her that they were "meant to be together."

Mary's story

"Mary" is a composite drawn from several sources. Anyone who has suffered in an authoritarian personal relationship will recognize the behaviors:

For Mary, it was love at first sight. She was impressed by Jeff's extrovert personality – he just walked up to her table in the cafeteria, and, completely ignoring her friends, fixed his eye on her as he said, "You are the most attractive woman I have ever seen. I mean *ever*."

Mary had escaped a bad relationship just weeks before, after she found that her fiancée had been cheating on her. He had seemed bored with her for some time, so Jeff's steady stream of compliments was welcome.

Their first date was a movie, and Mary was a little startled at Jeff's rudeness to the usher on their way in. They went on to have dinner at an expensive restaurant. Mary had to pay, because Jeff claimed to have forgotten his wallet.

Jeff was bursting with plans and schemes, but none of them ever came to fruition. He took a loan out to start an Internet business, but lost the money at the racetrack. Mary wondered if he needed help for a gambling addiction, but Jeff was angry at the suggestion and said that perhaps she needed help not to poke her nose into his business.

Whenever they went into a shop, Jeff couldn't leave without lifting a trophy. Mary was embarrassed by his shoplifting, but her attempts to change his behavior met with derision, and he never showed the slightest remorse. He said that the shopkeepers deserved to lose goods; that he was "testing their security"; and that insurance would always pay the difference, so no one really lost out. "People who aren't careful deserve to be hoodwinked," he said.

Mary was usually cautious, so Jeff's frequent risk-taking caused her anxiety. For instance, Jeff usually put his foot down to drive through a red light. One day when he almost hit another car, which shook Mary to the core, he seemed euphoric. He said that she was "no fun."

Jeff boasted about his own smarts and savagely ridiculed anyone who bested him in argument. Rather than rebutting their disagreeable ideas, he would make derogatory comments about their appearance or their past.

One day, Mary realized that Jeff had been checking her phone. When she pointed this out, he at first denied any knowledge, and then said that he had wanted to make sure she wasn't cheating on him. He claimed that he had been badly hurt in a previous relationship; Mary felt sorry for him.

Within weeks, the charming mask slipped, and Jeff often flew into a rage without the slightest provocation. Mary spent hours making an elaborate meal. Jeff spat out the first mouthful and threw the plate on the floor, while insulting Mary's culinary abilities.

One evening they met three of her girlfriends, and Mary was horrified at the slighting comments that Jeff made to them about her. She stopped taking Jeff to meet her friends, because he was so rude to them. He told her that her friends were selfish idiots. Her friends tried to warn her, but Mary was devoted to Jeff and confessed their suspicions to him. Jeff was furious and insisted that if she loved him, she would drop all contact with them. Mary was now isolated socially.

Jeff's persistent complaints eroded Mary's self-esteem. He criticized everything: her clothes, her hair, her taste in movies; he said she was "simple-minded" and "incompetent" and she began to believe him and began to make even more mistakes.

One day, Mary came home from work early to find her beloved cat Thomas strung up by the paws and hanging from a light-fitting. Jeff readily admitted stringing Thomas up and said, "So you care more about a stupid cat than you do about me?"

Jeff was rude to her parents, who several times tried to warn her. At Jeff's request, Mary stopped seeing them and was only allowed to phone them when Jeff could listen in on the conversation. One night her father made a hostile comment about Jeff, so Jeff delivered an ultimatum: Mary had to choose between him and her parents.

Jeff lounged about or half-heartedly pursued his next money-making scheme. Mary ended up supporting him and taking on his bank loan. She worked long hours, but when she came home had to cook and clean. Jeff insisted that she cleaned the house every day. His clothes had to be ironed and folded. If she made a mistake (and she always did) Jeff tipped all the clothes on the floor, forcing her to wash, iron and fold them again.

In a temper tantrum, Jeff threatened to hit her. She locked herself in the bathroom shaking in fear. Jeff then cajoled her with flattery and apologized. He swore that he would never do it again, and called Mary: "My angel. The only thing that makes life worth living." Within a few days, Mary was locked quivering in the bathroom again.

Mary's world grew ever smaller, until all that she could think about was Jeff's well-being. She was very lucky, because her father had Jeff investigated and found that he had a string of convictions for petty crime and had jumped bail. Mary was furious when she found that her dad had reported Jeff to the police. Jeff was arrested, charged with a string of new offences and sentenced to prison. It took several months before she spoke to her dad again, but eventually the enchantment broke, and Mary realized she had been captivated by a malignant narcissist.

Signs of a coercive partner:
- boasting
- rudeness in public (particularly to service staff)
- scrounging
- narcissism and self-involvement

- fantastic schemes and unfinished projects
- financially irresponsible, wasting money
- unnecessary jealousy
- possessiveness
- anger, criticism and blame
- petty theft and antisocial behavior
- belief that others deserve hurt or harm
- risk-taking

Acts of a coercive partner:
- spying
- charming compliments alternating with criticism of personal tastes and habits
- demands for sympathy
- public putdowns
- false apologies
- criticism of friends, family and allies
- isolation from friends, family and allies
- demand for financial support
- petty rules
- gaslighting
- punishments
- threats of violence
- violence
- torture and sadism

the many faces of control

Coercive control has many faces, but only one intention: the manipulator comes to control every possible aspect of a partner's life, turning it into a living hell.

As Evan Stark points out in his *Coercive Control*, women are most often the targets of coercive control, in large part because of our male-dominated society. Because of this imbalance, the problem of violence towards men in intimate relationships still tends to be swept under the carpet. In 2002, Peter McBride was stabbed to death by his girlfriend, Sonia Wallace. McBride had endured eight years of physical violence, always pretending that he had hurt himself in accidents rather than blaming Wallace. It perhaps reflects the social prejudice against abused men that Wallace was able to plead to a manslaughter charge and served only 21 months for the killing.[239]

duping the professionals

Tragically, coercive control extends to children and children can be influenced so powerfully that even trained professionals can be influenced in such a way that they miss the signs; even obvious signs. Victoria Climbié was seven when her parents sent her to Europe from the Ivory Coast, believing that she would benefit from a European education. She stayed with her

great-aunt Marie-Thérèse Kouao, who told church authorities that the child was "possessed by an evil spirit". The great-aunt's boyfriend, Carl Manning, said the girl was Satan.

Victoria Climbié

Victoria's great-aunt even reported her boyfriend for sexually abusing the child, but despite a hospital admission and several referrals to social services, professionals simply noted that she was a "ray of sunshine" with a smile that "lit up the room" – and took no action to save her from the daily violent abuse she suffered. Victoria had been so severely manipulated that she was able to convince professionals to take no action. To cite the official report, "In the end, Victoria died of organ failure consequent to at least 128 injuries and severe neglect, including sleeping each night enclosed in a black plastic bag containing her urine and feces. Her great aunt and boyfriend were convicted of murder … the discrepancy between events and Victoria's affect openly amazed many people, but was not considered a warning sign."[240]

We must be aware of the signs of coercive control, if we are to minimize it in our society. An important part of this is accepting the evidence in front of our eyes, rather than justifying or excusing it without further investigation.

parental alienation

Parental alienation is another common form of coercive control. After separation, one parent will sometimes prevent any connection between the children and their other parent. A thoroughly negative view of the absent parent will be created, and the child's unwanted behavior will be compared to that parent ("You're just like your father/mother").

Years later, a now adult child may find that the absent parent's communication was blocked. Presents, cards, and letters have been destroyed or hidden to give the child the idea that they were not loved. This can cause life-long devastation: believing that your own parent rejected you is a hard burden to carry.

adolescent vulnerability

Adolescents are especially vulnerable to systematic thought reform. They are undergoing profound physical changes and will respond dramatically to changes in their social life. It is vital to belong, and many youngsters take a dangerous path because it is a normal aspect of society. Indeed, most adolescents even commit petty crimes during that transition. Adolescence is a time of transition for all primate species.[241]

modern initiations

At the point of entry into a group there is often an initiation. Cultures throughout the world initiate children into adult society. Christians may be "confirmed" in their faith at the onset of puberty. Jewish children undergo a Bar- or Bat-mitzvah. Traditional societies around the world have their own versions, from the Australian Aborigine to the Arizona Apache.

The rites of passage are specific and deliberate, and it is hoped that the child is helped into adulthood. The caprice of childhood gives way to familial and social duty. In many traditional societies, boys are frightened into fearlessness by grueling tests of their physical and psychological endurance. They leave the world of childhood to become men.

Such initiations confirm the moral rules of the society, but those rules are not universally shared. So, for instance, in many societies, female genital mutilation is practiced. To most of us in the West this practice is intolerably cruel. It has no medical benefit and often seals the fate of women in male-dominated societies. It is a cruel way to force girls into subservience.

Initiation is found in many groups, often as a series of steps, levels or grades. The Freemasons and Rosicrucians climb a ladder of degrees. However, it is often the first initiation into a group that is most significant. It indicates the adoption of a new identity. So, religious novices accept a new name to become a new person. This will also be found during gang initiations where the old pre-gang self is rejected.

Masonic groups have an equivalent in the fraternal societies of colleges in the US. For most students, college is the transition from family into society. Fraternities and sororities are a hugely powerful force. These groups usually adopt Greek letters for their names – like Phi Delta Kappa – so it is called "Greek life".

Membership of a sorority or fraternity is often a lifetime commitment. All of the alumni of a given fraternity or sorority will help one another in a brotherly or sisterly way. Like the Freemasons these groups are "old-boy" or "old-girl" networks, which raises questions about preferential treatment based upon acquaintance rather than merit.

Membership is certainly significant: 75% of US Congressmen and 40% of Congresswomen belong to fraternal societies – most famously Yale University's Skull and Bones. This dwarfs the 2% of such network members in the general society.

Fraternities and sororities are notorious for the use of "hazing". Students have been severely hurt and even killed during these antics. The BBC documentary *Frat Boys* included both a young woman who had been raped at a fraternity party and a young man – Terrence Bennett – who had been branded – with a red-hot branding iron – and almost died.[242] Bennett claims that he was beaten with boat paddles and urinated on before members of Tau Kappa Epsilon branded him.[243] Beatings and humiliation are commonplace, along with the consumption of dangerous amounts of alcohol.

During "Hell Week" at Lenoir-Rhyne University, Harrison Kowiak, an athletic 19-year-old, was blindfolded and urged to run

Harrison Kowiak

across a field in the middle of the night, while frat members football-tackled him and other prospects, as they searched for "sacred rocks". Kowiak suffered fatal brain damage during this ordeal, and his parents sued the young men who were involved in his death, eventually settling out of court in 2012.[244] At least 22 students have died in an eight-year period in similar incidents.

The American Association of Universities has published a study showing that one in four young women report unwanted sexual contact at college, while one in eight reports a serious sexual offence. It is estimated that frat boys are three times more likely to commit such offences than their peers in normal society. As one example, in 2015, Syracuse University suspended or expelled 16 students for sexual misconduct.

Hazing can be seen as simply youthful hijinks – but there are transformative potentials in the extreme behavior. As one frat boy put it, the intention is to "break these guys down – find out what we can do to build them up into better men." These words are a sinister echo of the thought reform ideas of communist China. The question is whether hard-drinking promiscuity and social advantage through connections does actually make "better men". There are far better ways of inculcating team spirit.

While fraternal societies own $3 billion worth of campus housing, and their alumni contribute 75% of the donations to private universities, it will be difficult to change this culture of thought reform, but 44 states have now criminalized hazing, and there are many cases in the US courts against fraternal societies and their members. There are also on-line resources, such as hazingprevention.org.[245]

Coercive control readily becomes institutionalized and those affected come to accept domineering behavior in the workplace, even when it violates their human rights. In the UK, in 2016, a parliamentary committee accused the retailer Sports Direct of "Victorian" practices and compared the company to state workhouses of that era, which were labor camps for the poor. MPs asserted that the company has failed to treat its members as "human beings". Union officials told the committee that one woman had given birth in a toilet at work, because she was afraid to ask for the day off.[246]

It is hard to believe that such practices continue into the 21st century, but, as the documentary *The Corporation* points out, businesses are legally forbidden to do anything beyond enriching their shareholders, so sometimes have the ethics of a psychopath. Corporate law has no place for compassion. At least the trade union was able to persuade the government to investigate.

According to the parliamentary committee, Sports Direct used coercive control to violate the rights of its workers.

faith-based medical neglect

In the 1840s, hypnotist Phineas Quimby began to develop the ideas that would become the New Thought Movement. His central assertion was that all disease is caused by faulty beliefs. His most famous patient was Mary Baker Eddy, who founded the Christian Science Church on Quimby's principles.

Many systems of belief have developed this notion further: that unhappiness and pain are caused by a lack of faith, and that medical conditions should be treated by prayer or "right thinking". In the 20th century, Ron Hubbard adopted this belief for Scientology – although unlike Christian Scientists, Scientologists are generally allowed to visit medical doctors (though the practice is discouraged).

The notion that an individual can re-arrange the universe by thought has resurfaced in the Law of Attraction and *The Secret*. In all such systems, the victim is blamed – even when they clearly suffer from a genetic condition or have been exposed to a virulent bacterium or virus.

Those who fall ill, or fail to be perfectly cheerful, are considered sinful or even demon-possessed in some groups. Scientology attributes ill health and unhappiness to connection with anti-Scientologists, and Mark Twain criticized Mary Baker Eddy for similar assertions – indeed, he said that her followers were "slaves".[247]

Jehovah's Witnesses have a complex and ever-changing policy regarding blood transfusions, derived from a reading of scripture. As a consequence, members of this sizeable organization die every day through refusal to allow transfusions. This is especially painful when the patients are children, whose parents refuse them treatment. In more enlightened countries, a court can overrule the parents' decision and save the child.

learning how to resist influence

My friend Lady Daphne Vane once said that we take in influence with our mother's milk. It is a good point. There may be some susceptibility in our genes, but, as there is nothing we can do about that retroactively, we have to concentrate on nurture.

Critical thinking skills are a part of the puzzle. Taking time on our own to think, and talking things over with people we're close to and trust is important. The Internet provides all sorts of information, but we need to teach our kids how to assess that information.

The tricks that are used to create false certainty through emotional responses, found in Yuval Laor's work, need to enter the curriculum, as do Ira Chaleff's intelligent disobedience and courageous followership.

A childhood in a supportive and encouraging environment – with a secure attachment to care-givers – goes a long way towards resisting influence. However, those of us who had the good fortune of such an environment may be too trusting, and so easily taken in by unscrupulous people. It's time to take a look at the traits of those people: the human predators.

recommended reading:

Patricia McKinsey Crittenden, *Raising Parents: Attachment, representation, and treatment.*
Evan Stark, *Coercive Control: How Men Entrap Women in Personal Life.*

15
the human predator

"You don't seem like a bad man."
"That's what makes me so good at it" ~ Nicolas Cage in *Matchstick Men*.

Different sources have different definitions for the varieties of low-empathy personality. The common terms psychopath and sociopath are no longer found in the American Psychiatric Association's Diagnostic and Statistical Manual (DSM), which is used around the globe as a yardstick for mental illnesses and personality disorders.

DSM 5 lists several low-empathy personality disorders: anti-social, borderline and narcissistic. I will use the term "human predator" or simply "predator" to cover both anti-social and narcissistic personality disorders. Borderlines are part social and part anti-social, so are often predatory.

Hervey Cleckley was the first to give a list of characteristics for the diagnosis of psychopathy (as he termed it) in his 1941 book, *The Mask of Sanity*. The term "psychopath" was first used a hundred years before, meaning literally "suffering mind". Study of low- empathy, selfish and aggressive types increased markedly after World War One, when it was realized that about a fifth of veterans hospitalized for mental difficulties had pre-existing anti-social conditions before they were sent to war.

While there is significant agreement about the condition, there are experts who feel that the considerable variation among those labeled as psychopaths makes any definition imprecise. However, our interest is in the behaviors, not in diagnosis or treatment, so we can safely examine the characteristics that many experts associate with this range of personality disorders. It is the predatory actions of these people that we need to recognize: whatever might be the correct diagnostic designation, we want to protect ourselves and those we love from harmful people.

Predatory traits can diminish with time. Psychologist Terrie Moffitt has shown that most adolescents will at some time commit criminal acts, but, unless their behavior is reinforced by punishment, the majority will become more social with time.[248] Our concern is to proof society from predatory attitudes and behaviors.

"If I wasn't studying psychopaths in prison, I'd do it at the stock exchange."

~Robert Hare

In the 1970s, Canadian psychologist Robert Hare further developed Cleckley's diagnostic criteria to create the Psychopathy Checklist for use by qualified professionals. In his book *Without Conscience*,[249] Hare explained his criteria for a diagnosis of psychopathy. He maintains that psychopaths are emotionally glib; that they can be very charming but have a grandiose self-image, making them boastful; and, because they are easily bored, they constantly search for stimulation.

Those considered to be psychopaths are cunning, manipulative and compulsively deceptive. They have no remorse and feel no guilt. Their emotions are shallow, and they lack empathy. They tend to be parasitic, contributing nothing of real worth to society. Such people do not attach emotionally – they do not feel love as others do, only self-regard – their lack of emotional attachment and need for constant stimulation tends to make them sexually promiscuous. Psychopaths are impulsive, and take no responsibility for their actions.

In short, those labeled psychopaths are utterly selfish and lack any feeling or concern for others. They are bullies who delight in humiliating those around them. They abuse trust and have no conscience. They deceive everyone they meet. They are particularly good at deflecting criticism and they cannot stand anyone else being praised – they have to be seen as the best and compete shamelessly to be the center of attention. They tend to be control freaks, and will not allow anyone around to control anything if they can possibly stop them. Psychopaths are also authoritarian by nature, and *they want total authority.*

As with other psychological disorders, we have to generalize according to symptoms, but the general category known by the labels "psychopath", "sociopath", "malignant narcissist" or "anti-social personality disorder", is useful in understanding predatory people who have no concern for the welfare or well-being of others.

Hare differentiates the "sociopath" as the milder form of psychopath.[250] While perhaps three per cent of men are psychopaths, in Hare's sense, and one per cent of women, there is a much higher proportion of sociopaths, which would include narcissists.

We owe the term "malignant narcissist" to Erich Fromm, who also described the "benign" narcissist.[251] Havelock Ellis introduced the term "narcissist" to psychology to mean people who only love themselves and show this "self-love" through masturbation.[252] Freud distorted the meaning to mean people who brag and boast. As Fromm points out, narcissists are actually incapable of love and demand approval, adulation, and obedience from others because they lack a fully formed self. Properly speaking, the word "narcissist" is inaccurate.

Benign narcissists need constant approval but are not malevolent; malignant narcissists are malevolent. They are human predators.

Unfortunately, the majority of people fit Fromm's description of the benign narcissist: keeping up with the Joneses; acquiring status symbols; needing approval for their behavior. Professor Jane McGregor calls such people "apaths" and says they make up about 60% of the population. She asserts that sociopaths/psychopaths recruit such apaths to harm the small quantity of empaths in our society and restrict their positive effect.[253] A small quantity of human predators can have a drastic effect, which is why spotting and restraining them is so important.

The word "psychopath" conjures images of serial killers, but thankfully, homicidal psychopaths are a tiny minority. Some psychopaths are violent, but most focus on controlling the people around them psychologically.

Leaders of authoritarian groups most often fit into the malignant narcissistic variant of the anti-social personality – they are self-aggrandizing, envious and lacking in empathy. Such people can be highly successful in business, because of their ruthlessness – Robert Maxwell is a good example. They don't spend time worrying about environmental, physical or emotional damage or, indeed, any harm that may come from their actions. Narcissists love power, so they are often found in the judiciary, the police, the military, and especially in politics. Our society has no safeguards against this personality type, and their glib charm at times allows them to achieve tremendous power, even in a democratic society.

the authoritarian leader

The leader of an authoritarian group may not actually be a narcissist, but if they are not it is likely that they are in the thrall of a psychopath or suffer from the borderline personal-

Robert Maxwell, press baron and narcissist

ity disorder, which means that they can be both highly positive and highly destructive. Some investigators divide the narcissistic personality into two categories: vulnerable and grandiose. The "vulnerable" type believe that they are special and want others to applaud their special talents, but they are neither competent nor attractive. They are prone to angry and violent outbursts if their status is not recognized. They are introverted and self-absorbed. The "grandiose" type have more confidence: they have an unshakeable belief in their superiority, and they want everyone to know about it. They are pompous, but they can also be charming.[254]

Erich Fromm used the term "malignant narcissist" to differentiate psychopathic narcissists from exhibitionists. Many performers are narcissistic – or self-obsessed – but they do not exploit those around them.[255] Dan Shaw used the term "traumatic narcissism" for his fine book on the subject.[256]

In the worst cases, the psychopath rises to national power. Without adequate checks, such people can cause devastation. Mao, Hitler and Stalin exemplify the danger of psychopathy. Dictatorship is the pinnacle of megalomania – whether it be seized, elected or inherited.

Powerful people often become powerful because they long for power.

Self-importance is a terrible drug: power encourages the production of testosterone – a hormone associated with aggression – in both men and women, driving a lust for ever more power and, in turn, the demonstration of more aggression in some people.

human predators

Throughout history, people have elevated and served psychopaths. The tribal leaders who created the first kingdoms may well have been megalomaniac psychopaths.[257] History catalogues the rise of tyrants who maintained their bloodline without concern for merit. Only with the appearance of democracy in the last few centuries has this model of behavior been challenged, but democracy too has allowed monsters to take charge – both Hitler and Mussolini gained their initial power through the ballot box.

Why do people vote for vain, deceitful, selfish and self-aggrandizing leaders? Should we submit all prospective political candidates to a psychopathy test? Professor Tony Maden, an expert on psychopathy, has suggested that we should take far more care in understanding not simply the policies but also the personalities of potential leaders. If the world had listened to the Norwegian psychiatrist who labeled Hitler a psychopath in 1933 – the year he came to power – his megalomaniac ambitions might have been contained. *In an uncertain world, we are drawn to those who boast certainty.*

As we have seen, among the most alarming statistics of the Third Reich is the number of medical doctors who joined the Nazi party and carried out the murder of almost 200,000 disabled patients. No other profession flocked to the Nazi standard in such numbers – forty-five per cent – even though these were ostensibly the professionals best qualified to understand the delusive nature of Hitler's pronouncements.

Those who serve predatory leaders become predators. Even the best-meaning and most empathetic people can be persuaded to lie, cheat, steal, to humiliate, punish and abuse others under the sway of a predator. They become "weaponized empaths": under the influence of the predator they will become selfish and ape the deceptive, manipulative behavior of the predator, who has become their leader in both thought and action. Morality is sacrificed for the good of the cause.

Believers in a cause can become authoritarian, because they are convinced of the urgency of that cause. Both the leader and the followers are "authoritarian". The leaders believing themselves to be superior and the followers depending upon what they believe to be a leader's superiority. As Shakespeare said, some are born great, some achieve greatness, and some have greatness thrust upon them. Some authoritarians are born, but some adopt the behaviors of others. The very best people can become dangerous authoritarians when they use their intelligence to bolster erroneous convictions.[258]

Authoritarian leaders are predators and authoritarian followers are prey. In a sane and just society, we are neither predators nor prey. There is both "dominance" and "prestige" leadership in our society. Dominance leadership is authoritarian, where prestige leadership is compassionate and consensual.[259]

authoritarianism and psychopaths

Authoritarianism is a way of being for psychopaths and narcissists. In an authoritarian marriage, one partner will subject the other to impossible, petty rules and punish the inevitable failure to meet those rules. The same is true within authoritarian groups, where the leadership sets up standards that are humanly impossible to achieve, and then derides the failure to achieve those standards.

The coerced spouse, the humiliated gang member, the abused child and the authoritarian group member will usually come to accept their own failure rather than the impossibility of the rules. Everything good is the gift of the predator; everything bad is the fault of the follower.

As with psychopaths, narcissistic predators have no concern for the feelings of those around them. Nor do they have any concern for their well-being, their health or their sanity. Malignant narcissists are cold-hearted, but they are also good at pretending, so they can mimic feeling and concern effectively. Just catch them when they don't know you are looking, and you will see the hidden grin that mocks the victim of their latest emotional demand.

Predators make nasty comments about others. They use *triangulation*, inventing gossip about a target. They will undermine their victims with gaslighting, making them think that they are at fault.

The most striking feature of the narcissist is their charm. Many narcissists excel at flattery. Conversely, those at the positive end of the empathetic scale are naturally encouraging and supportive. Such people can be positively saintly in their concern for others, a property which is convincingly imitated by human predators (especially "saintly narcissists").

Where an empathetic person will offer compliments to make others feel better, a predator will use compliments to gain influence and control. As a general rule, it is best to add a pinch of salt to any compliments given by strangers. By now, we all know that salespeople are trained to lure us with a smile and praise. Of course, empathetic people will also approach in a friendly way, so we should not simply give a cold shoulder to all comers – nor should we give them our money, our time, or our promises.

The simplest response is to leave if the talk turns to immediate commitment to an unknown product, cause or individual. If you feel in the slightest suspicious, leave the conversation and think about what happened. Check with your friends to see what they think. Find out about the person who approached you through social media and search engines.

It is hard to develop *friendly distrust*, but trust should be earned. When we recognize a predator, we should make others aware of their behavior – if that behavior is excessive – but we must be careful to describe that behavior accurately.

It is unclear how predatory behavior develops, and it is easy to fall into polarized thinking about the origins of the condition. There are important gradations of psychopathic and narcissistic behavior, but all types are afflicted by a lack of empathy for others and a lack of remorse.

Some are born predators, some acquire predatory behavior, and some have predatory behavior thrust upon them. Nature and nurture are both involved. There are successful therapeutic interventions for narcissistic personality disorder, but the severe forms of psychopathy are still beyond intervention.

It is a mistake to believe that the psychopath is inevitably dangerous. The popular TV show *Dexter* put forward the idea of a socially responsible serial killer. We could dismiss this apparent contradiction if Dexter were not based on a real live serial killer – Manuel Pardo – who

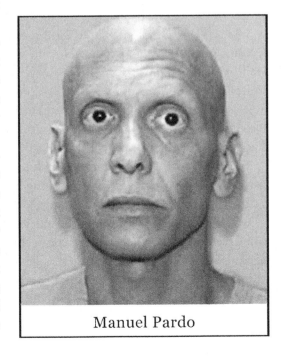

Manuel Pardo

was a policeman and only killed drug dealers, whom he considered evil.

However, Manuel Pardo was a bad man in all areas of his life, where the character played by Michael C Hall is friendly if unempathetic at times. If nothing else, such a man would have to hide this part of his nature from everyone, so could never be open and honest – characteristics of the social personality. We must not condemn everyone who is low on empathy because of their condition or start any witch-hunts. Punishment does not help predators, but those who cannot change their ways must be restrained from harming others. They should still retain all of their human rights even if imprisoned. There is no need for us to behave like psychopaths.

bullying

Putting aside diagnostic criteria, perhaps the most important aspect of authoritarian behavior is bullying. Towards the end of my time in Scientology, I hired a former high-ranking executive of the group to help with my artists' agency. One week, because my wife had made no sales, the executive took her into a tiny room and screamed his head off at her. I found out later that he was inches away from her face. He yelled that she was deliberately "suppressing" me and had "evil intentions". I hovered outside the door trapped in cognitive dissonance: he was a graduate of Scientology's vaunted Flag Executive Briefing Course and a former aide to Ron Hubbard, yet he was behaving in a brutal and callous way, completely out of character with the man I knew.

It was three days before I challenged him. Scientology is supposed to run on clear, written instructions, so I asked where this procedure was explained. I had expected a robust defense, so I was surprised when he slumped forward with his head in his hands and began to cry. He told me that the technique was called a "severe reality adjustment" and there was nothing in the policy of Scientology describing it. I asked him where he had learned the technique, and he said, "Hubbard did it to us". I later found that this is a daily practice in Scientology's Sea Organization.

This blazing destructive rage is intended to humiliate and subdue any disagreement. I am sure that it is an essential part of Scientology's slave-making apparatus. It can take years to restore eroded self-esteem after such predatory behavior. *We don't have to make a diagnosis: anyone who yells insults at you is by definition being anti-social.*

Neuroscientist James Fallon was surprised to find that his own brain scan was consistent with that of the serial killers whose brains he was studying. He also found that he had gene markers associated with psychopathy, and his family history revealed seven murderers – including the infamous Lizzie Borden (though Borden was actually acquitted).

Despite his genes and his brain, Fallon is not predatory, which has led him to coin the term "pro-social psychopath". While this should lead to hesitation about using brain scans to identify psychopaths – as Tony Blair's government suggested for UK children – it should not deter us from identifying predatory behavior in the effort to help both society and the psychopath, regardless of brain scans or genes.

empathy overload

Recent studies have pointed to empathy overload in the caring professions. Exposed to too much suffering, nurses, doctors and therapists can collapse under the strain. When people vent, they often simply feel worse: it seems that there is no talking cure for this emotional contagion. One solution to this problem has come from an unusual source: diagnosed psychopaths. It may be possible to learn something from their lack of empathy.

With empathy we feel another's pain, which can be overwhelming. Matthieu Ricard has suggested that we learn compassion instead: "Compassion is feeling for and not with the other". The compassionate person does not actually feel the same feelings as the person who is being helped. Tania Singer at the Max Planck Institute in Leipzig is leading efforts to apply this notion and the lessons learned from psychopaths to overloaded health workers. This came while President Barack Obama was calling for greater training in empathy.[260] Sometimes too much empathy is the problem. Yale psychologist Paul Bloom has written a useful discussion called *Against Empathy: The Case for Rational Compassion.*[261]

While we must be careful not to label anyone wrongly, it is vital that we learn to recognize predators, thus limiting the damage they cause throughout society. We can at least distance ourselves from such people and restrict their influence. Perhaps one day we will be able to cure them. Until then, for the sake of all concerned, we all need to know who they are and how they behave. Imagine a world with no predatory police officers, judges, or politicians. It seems a Utopian dream, but it is already possible to identify the psychopathic brain, and it might be right to exclude people who are most likely to lack conscience from certain professions.

There are professions where a steely-eyed detachment is a positive trait. For instance, after studying the Bay of Pigs invasion and other examples of groupthink, Irving Janis suggested that all decision-making bodies should employ a devil's advocate to argue against every proposition. No one is better equipped than a pro-social psychopath for this task, because they will not bow down to the group to fit in. If western governments had been able to listen to pro-social psychopaths, rather than bowing to groupthink, the invasion of Iraq might never have happened.

narcissism and success

Attitudes towards narcissism have shifted. In a review of 42 US presidents, Ashley Watts and her colleagues at Emory University determined that those presidents considered the most successful tended to exhibit grandiose narcissism. These individuals were more persuasive, better at crisis management and risk assessment, and initiated more legislation, though they were also held to be impulsive bullies.[262] But perhaps some of these men extended their narcissism to the entire nation, so furthered progress towards equal rights and a more democratic society.

Craig Malkin, who lectures at Harvard Medical School questions the Narcissistic Personality Inventory which is standardly used to measure narcissism. He designed a new instrument, the Narcissistic Spectrum Scale, with his colleague, Professor Stuart Quick, which may be a more accurate assessment.[263]

Malkin offers a spectrum of narcissim which he describes as a measure of "feeling special". At the zero end of the spectrum is the "echoist", who has little or no self-esteem, at 10, the far end of the spectrum, is the narcissist. Malkin posits a midpoint at 5: the somewhat oxymoronic "healthy narcissist". It is perhaps more accurate to say that those at 0 and 10 have no self-esteem, but at 0 they hide from attention and at 10 they demand attention (in the form of adulation). In each case, this can be seen as a failure to develop a mature personality.

Simon Baron-Cohen and his colleagues at Cambridge University have devised the Empathy Quotient to measure empathy.[264] If we are to solve the pressing problems of warfare, economic instability and environmental degradation, we need to find a balance between the empathetic and the effective. The solution may well come by building teams that contain a range of personality types and using the talents of people with both high and low empathy.

A great deal has been discovered about human predators, but little of this information is taught in our educational systems. Next, we look at this failure and why this information should be broadly known.

recommended reading:

James Fallon, *The Psychopath Inside: A Neuroscientist's Personal Journey into the Dark Side of the Brain.*
Robert Hare, *Without Conscience: the disturbing world of the psychopaths among us.*
Simon Baron-Cohen, *Zero Degrees of Empathy: A New Theory of Human Cruelty and Kindness.*
David Robson, *The Intelligence Trap: Why smart people do stupid things and how to make wiser decisions*

16
understanding the past to
find the way forward

"In the light of what we have learned recently about animal behavior in general, and human behavior in particular, it has become clear that control through the punishment of undesirable behavior is less effective, in the long run, than control through the reinforcement of desirable behavior by rewards, and that government through terror works on the whole less well than government through the non-violent manipulation of the environment and of the thoughts and feelings of individual men, women and children ... In *1984* the lust for power is satisfied by inflicting pain; in *Brave New World*, by inflicting a hardly less humiliating pleasure." ~ Aldous Huxley, *Brave New World Revisited*, 1957.

It is not enough to know that many advertisers, spin doctors, authoritarian groups and terrorist recruiters have hidden agendas; we need to know how those agendas work. There is a developed understanding of these mechanisms in psychology, but it somehow has not entered the public consciousness. Cognitive dissonance remains a foreign term to the vast majority of people. Children learn about George Washington or Queen Victoria, but almost nothing about the fundamental principles of their own behavior, or how to form good relationships.

Literacy and numeracy, once considered only the first steps of learning, have assumed a central position. The skills of rhetoric – where students learn to analyze and evaluate ideas, so that they can be articulated rationally – have long since vanished from the curriculum. On a positive note, the critical thinking movement has shifted the emphasis of education, encouraging students to participate in the lifelong adventure of learning, rather than instilling a catalogue of facts to be disgorged at examinations; however, progress is slow.

For years, the Program for International Student Assessment's (PISA) surveys have shown that education is best when put in the hands of creative teachers, rather than fixed into a curriculum. The most successful systems in academic terms – in Finland, Shanghai and South Korea – have also minimized testing.

Declines in educational achievement in the UK and the US have come alongside a significant *increase* in testing. In 2014 in the UK, without consultation, Michael Gove, then Minister for Education, shifted the whole system back to examination only, ending years of "continuous assessment." The opinions of teachers who may well have spent years teaching a child were put aside. This was disrespectful of teachers, who have been reduced to following the same tedious curriculum year on year. We need creativity in our children, and we won't achieve that until we allow teachers to enjoy their work again.

There is a conflict between those who believe we must be constrained into social conformity and those who believe education should instill curiosity and creative originality. The paradigm has yet to shift, but we are moving towards a less brutal and more considerate society in the "developed" countries, and that will certainly allow us to better uncover and resist hidden influence.

the age of anxiety

Each generation develops its own spirit or *zeitgeist*. Clear distinctions between art as promotion and "art for art's sake" were first made in the 20th century. Painting, for instance, evolved during the early Renaissance to inspire religious belief. The portrait exalted the patrons of the arts – the rulers of states and religions soon took center stage. Humanism was born and promoted throughout the arts.

The Reformation gave birth to a critique of social behaviors, which led to the Enlightenment and a move away from the inherited dictatorships of old Europe. The Romantics created a new identification with the majestic forces of nature and questioned the regimentation of society. The Expressionist movement took a negative view of humanity, which seemed to be borne out by the horrors of two world wars. Poet WH Auden dubbed the 20th century the "age of anxiety", and *angst* remains the watchword of the arts into this century, where the concept has now displaced the aesthetically pleasing object.

As the new shoots of "high" art faltered after the carnage of World War One, popular new forms swept the world – largely originating in the US, which "coca-colonized" the world with successive waves of jazz, blues, rock and roll, and cinema. Even the most sophisticated artists became agents of propaganda – Picasso's dove design for the Communist International is a direct example.

Picasso's dove

The mood of a culture is determined by its artists, and thus, by those who promote their work. The most popular work reflects the cultural mood – so TV dramas have casually taken on the role of informing society. Today, the most skillful writers are employed by Hollywood or the streaming networks. Playwrights like Tom Stoppard or Christopher Hampton turned from intellectual stage plays to Hollywood blockbusters (including *Shakespeare in Love* and *Dangerous Liaisons*). Comedy Central and HBO have also become a vital source for political information. In the UK, a deep examination of the Iraq Invasion came from satirists Bremner, Bird and Fortune, in *Between Iraq and a Hard Place*.

In a strange twist of fate, conceptual art has achieved supremacy in the western world, promoted by the likes of Charles Saatchi, who became a patron while running a group of advertising agencies, which, among other achievements, brought Margaret Thatcher to political power.

The boundaries between high and low culture have eroded, especially with the enthusiastic adoption of marketing strategies in classical music and theatre. The work of psychologist Judith Rich Harris clearly shows that we develop our lifelong tastes and beliefs in early adolescence, influenced not so much by parents nor educators, but largely by our peer group.[265]

Most people will continue to listen to the music that captivated them in their teens and follow the values they adopted at that time. Those values come from popular culture. If we are to teach liberty and equality, we must turn education into an interactive, multiplayer game, rather than a fusty, obedience-driven obsession with SAT scores.

honest persuasion versus coercion

When Jemaah Islamiyah leader Nasir Abas was arrested in Indonesia, he braced himself for torture. Instead, Abas was persuaded to reveal his own inner turmoil about civilian casualties by a religious expert, not an interrogator. The security services effectively *counseled* Abas out of his fanatical affiliation. With his help, they rounded up most of the al-Qaeda related network in South East Asia, the world's most populous Muslim region. The group, responsible for the Bali bombings, has continued to lose support since declaring its allegiance to Daesh/ISIS. [266]

Despite its dreadful civil rights record, Indonesia's approach has been markedly different to that of the United States and its allies. The US has subjected hundreds of alleged terrorists to brutal and humiliating treatment, which, former President Obama admitted during his term, amounts to torture and a violation of international law.[267]

Though this aggressive policy may have foiled some terrorist plots, it has disseminated terror rather than containing it. There were less than 500 members in the four groups lumped together as Al Qaeda when the awful tragedy of 9/11 shocked the world. Currently, there are hundreds of thousands of Al Qaeda, Daesh/ISIS and Shia activists, many of whom joined up as a direct consequence of violent military action and reports of torture at "black sites".

talking with a fanatic

Shock tactics are counter-productive. However, with patience, most fanatics will reconsider even the most entrenched views, just as alcoholics, gamblers and other addicts can be persuaded to change without aggressive intervention. My long experience with authoritarian group members bears this out.

A safe setting without fear of physical or psychological torment allows a fanatic to examine fixed ideas. The counselor must have empathy for the beliefs, attitudes and behaviors of the subject, and a deep knowledge of the realities of the condition or affiliation.

Gradually, the member's own abiding doubts will surface. Then the deception and exploitation of the authoritarian relationship can be explored. Such interventions are comparable to the extensive and highly successful denazification process after WWII, and are relevant to anyone who has been subjected to an institutional experience or reduced to compliance by a manipulator. The template for such an intervention can be transferred to many other situations, including the de-radicalization of a terrorist.

For her master's dissertation in coercive control, psychiatrist Nicki Crowley argued that those of us with long experience in helping members of authoritarian cult groups could help to shape more successful approaches to deradicalization.[268] As yet, we have largely been ignored.

The next chapter shows how to be more aware of predators.

recommended reading:

Lalich and Tobias, *Take Back Your Life.*
Ken Robinson, *Creative Schools.*

17

bringing the living
back to life: from groupthink
to courageous followership [269]

"We can, if we so desire, refuse to co-operate with the blind forces that are propelling us. For the moment, however, the wish to resist does not seem to be very strong or very widespread." ~ Aldous Huxley, *Brave New World Revisited*, 1957.

Ten per cent of 12-year-olds in the US have been "medicated" for anxiety, hyperactivity or depression. Emeritus professor of neurology James Austin advocates meditation instead of medication. Improved concentration would undoubtedly benefit our attention-deficit society.

The meditation Professor Austin recommends is not the repetition of mantras, leading to euphoric self-hypnosis, but the Buddhist "mindfulness" meditation, where thoughts are quieted, and attention heightened. [270]

Unfortunately, the term "mindfulness" has become a buzzword, often recommended by people who have little understanding of meditation and its potential pitfalls. Meditation should be approached with care. Many groups call their hypnotic procedures "meditation". Many people are made anxious by meditation. This condition, called "relaxation induced anxiety", shows that it is important to couple meditative passivity with physical exercise. [271]

Former authoritarian group members often say that they wished they had listened to their intuition. It is a valid point. In speaking with former members, they all offer up red flags that they ignored: the long hours, the lack of external information, the derision towards critics, uniform dress codes, esoteric language, the leadership's obsession with money and praise. But the desire for enlightenment, heaven, a socialist workers' paradise, justice on earth, or even a loving relationship made them ignore that inner voice.

There is a paradox here: a vicar with an Oxford law degree once told me he had abandoned doctoral research where he had tried to differentiate whether such "intuition" or inspiration comes from God or the Devil. He could find no rational way of discerning, but rationality is the way to check our intuition, wherever it comes from.

If we pay close heed to our intuition, but test it against evidence, we shall be much safer in our daily life. Intuition itself is too prone to bias to be the sole means of testing anything. An experienced manipulator will quickly take over intuition, inducing phobia, guilt and/or disgust so that followers will "intuitively" accept ideas that do not stand up to rational examination.

I am convinced that evil is largely indoctrinated,[272] but that goodness is a personal decision. As James Fallon proves, even someone born with sociopathic tendencies can contribute positively to society. Good people take responsibility and change the world around them.

critical thinking is not inborn

Education should encourage disagreement as a foundation for critical thinking, rather than instilling compliance with untested authority. While teaching self-assurance and respectful behavior, we must constantly monitor the unquestionable assumptions of our cultural truisms, the holy cows of our belief systems.

Resistance to persuasion depends upon developing cool rationality, which necessitates the ability to quiet down emotional arousal, without losing a compassionate perspective. In this respect, new studies of secular meditation are very important.

In 2008, a replication of Milgram's classic compliance experiment showed that the significant difference between those who readily give shocks and those who refuse is a sense of responsibility for their actions. While the only answer to groupthink is individual accountability, western society is actually becoming ever more institutionalized. Studies show that compassion is in decline among students; we are being dehumanized in the welter of information. The value of religion – of pro-social religion – is its focus on compassion. In a secular society, we need to develop tolerance, compassion and concern for others; this is best for both society, and for the individual within society.

The new discipline of *courageous followership* – pioneered in the US – teaches responsible following, showing people how to amend their leader's behavior and so overcome our animal inclination to groupthink. Ira Chaleff, an originator of courageous followership, has summed up the philosophy in the title of his book, *Intelligent Disobedience*. He points to the example of guide dogs, which need to be able to refuse orders that will endanger the person they are helping. *We need better leaders, but that objective will only be achieved if we become responsible followers.*

As Alan Watts said, *"When you confer spiritual authority on another person, you must realize that you are allowing them to pick your pocket and sell you your own watch."*[273] The same is true for political authority.

An evolution in psychotherapy has moved away from endlessly revisiting past trauma – which tends either to reinforce that trauma or create false memories – to therapies which teach careful attention to our own thoughts and responses, so that we can develop new thoughts and better responses.

a real education

Education is the key to all of our influence problems. It would be relatively easy to add not simply critical thinking but an understanding of the tricks of the mind – as explained in this book – to the curriculum; however, this demands a fundamental paradigm shift. We have to create a comfortable learning environment where teachers do not feel compelled to use entrained control techniques.

To do this, we have to raise the status (and pay) of our teachers, at least in most western countries, and either make learning so much fun that children simply revel in it, or find a more effective way of dealing with disruption, or both. Online sites such as Khan Academy and Crash Course have proved immensely popular and point towards exciting, rather than dulling, curiosity.

In part, the difficulty is that we do not teach our children the skills of assertiveness. We must, in moving forward, encourage them to say, politely: "Hold on a minute. Why are we doing this?"

When I was at school, it was still considered quite normal to beat children. By the time my oldest son went to school, this practice had been outlawed, but teachers would still shout to maintain dominance. I'm happy to report a far more considerate attitude from my two youngest boys' teachers. The culture is changing.

In the traditional view, education is a transmission of knowledge from those who know to those who do not. While the teacher should have far more information about a subject, it is time to accept that we are all – students and teachers – engaged in learning, and a school is a community of learning for everyone concerned. Knowledge is fascinating, so it is terrible that so many children find school a wearying environment.

Children are taught that our knowledge of the world is unambiguous, but the truth is that we do not understand the world fully, and even the most secure ideas may change with further enquiry (which is the nature of science). Moreover, subjects are divided in school, as if geography, literature and history existed in separate worlds, when in fact they are tightly interrelated disciplines needed to better a student's full understanding. It is important to grasp the overlap between disciplines.

Traditionally, the teacher is seen as infallible, which drowns out dissent and encourages obedience. The purpose of education is seen by some as simply filling the student's head with facts, many of which will have no relevance in later life. It is much better to teach skills and approaches than streams of facts. *There is a significant difference between authority that is earned and authority that is imposed.* The first is expert authority, the second is rank authority. We all learn more readily in an environment where our teachers *show* their worth, rather than simply *insisting* upon it.

Thomas Edison used a 146-question test to determine who he would employ. The test included such questions as "Who is called the father of railroads in the US?" and "Who wrote the Star-Spangled Banner?". Einstein famously failed the Edison Test. He explained that if he needed to know the speed of light, he could look it up.

Bad education enforces unthinking obedience. Good education stimulates curiosity. A good teacher instills confidence, where a bad teacher heightens self-consciousness.[274]

whistle-blowers and believers

Fundamentalism is in blazing ascent. Claiming God's inspiration, militant *takfiris* wage *jihad* against *kafirs*. George W. Bush, as the leader of the free world, justified his violent response, claiming to be instructed by the very same God. Even the more secular UK was dragged in Bush's wake by a closet born-again Prime Minister, who preached the gospel of military intervention, deriding *peacekeeping* long before the conflict began. We need to be wary of hidden – or overtly dangerous – religious agendas.

Truth and reconciliation can provide closure for our cultural clashes and blood feuds. After any conflict, an independent tribunal should assign responsibility for atrocities. Otherwise, the cycle of brutality will continue endlessly. Both sides of any conflict should be examined openly and the blameworthy exposed.

This is not a matter of meting out punishment, but coming to terms with the past, and laying it to rest. Where injustice has been glossed over, resentment smolders for generations. The conflict in the Middle East is rooted in the policies of the French and British authorities, which took high-handed control after the dissolution of the Ottoman Empire, at the end of World War One. A significantly unfair and tyrannical society was created. Consider Lebanon, for instance, where the French authorities denied the vote to the non-Christian majority, or Iran, where an elected government was forced out by a western coup that re-instated the Shah.

We cannot simply draw a line in the sand and move forward, as Tony Blair once said. The trauma of the past needs to be expressed, so that it can be left behind. *Muslims will continue to be "radicalized" as long as their co-religionists are unfairly treated.*

To promote positive change, and overcome loyalty to bad leaders, we must also support whistle-blowers, rather than ruining their lives. The Russell Crowe movie *The Insider* is based upon the real-life story of Jeffrey Wigand, who exposed the tobacco industry's experiments to make tobacco more addictive, and paid dearly for his honorable stand. It is possible to overcome the herd instinct to *groupthink* and thereby make a better world.

resisting manipulation

As individuals, we can learn to quell emotional arousal to find rational solutions. Straightforward tools exist for recognizing ideologues and exploiters. Paul Ekman's pioneering methods of behavioral lie detection have long been used by US government agencies (and generated the amusing TV crime drama, *Lie to Me*). Ekman teaches a clear-minded examination of evidence, which is further enhanced by developing a questioning, devil's advocate position towards enthusiasts of every persuasion, from the eco-puritan to the advocate of peace-through-murder.

Researchers at the University of Cardiff have developed a system to grade the authenticity of evidence. Professor Harry Collins asks us to imagine the discovery of a terrorist gene. Right-wingers would demand birth control or sterilization. The media would carry scare stories. It is not impossible that a government would initiate a testing program (as we've seen, Tony Blair's UK Labor government suggested such testing for infant sociopaths, at the beginning of this century). It is better to treat all children fairly and with compassion, because that is the only known treatment for the sociopathic disorder. A study at Wisconsin's Mendota Juvenile Treatment Center confirms this view. Participants in their study committed far fewer crimes than those in the control group.[275]

Collins shows how to determine the authority of an expert and how to better construct evidence. To show how gullible even scientists can be, he even passed himself off as an accomplished physicist at a conference. Not one of the assembled scientists suspected his complete lack of credentials, even though he did nothing more than parrot their own words back to them.

We need to take time before committing ourselves. Today's "buy now" offer will continue until the goods are actually sold. We need to be in a calm frame of mind, because both optimism and pessimism are actually irrational. It is hard to reason when we are either too cheerful or too sad, so we should put off important decisions until we are in a less excited or distressed state.

Sleep deprivation is the "royal road" to compliance, according to one Guantanamo Bay torturer – captives were woken every hour, to make sure that they would never be fully awake: it is vitally important to your mental and physical health to make sure that you have enough sleep.

Proper nutrition is also vital. Extreme fasting endangers reasoning. The occasional day without food probably lengthens life, but too much fasting induces delusion. High-carbohydrate diets do not provide the nutrients necessary for the brain to function at its best.

Exercise to stay healthy, and to think better, but don't over-exercise – this causes high states through the release of opioids which act in the same way as opiate drugs like heroin.

Drugs and alcohol distort perception and interpretation. And that includes medical drugs, such as anti-depressants, anti-anxiety pills and painkillers. It is not enough not to operate machinery when under the influence: it is also necessary not to make any life-changing decisions. The same is true for the euphoria generated by the hypnotic techniques of authoritarian groups, and participation in group activities. It is wonderful to feel part of a group, but where a rock concert or an opera is usually a positive experience, this natural euphoria can easily be twisted into control by a manipulative group.

We must make clear distinctions between exploitative and ethical persuasion. While the former always uses deception, ethical persuasion is open and honest, and reveals all of the known information in a clearly accessible way.

In *The Art of Loving*,[276] Erich Fromm gives three extremely helpful spectrums. We can be "life-affirming" or "life-denying" – either pro-social or anti-social. We can be life-affirming in some ways and life-denying in others. The worst human predators control and devastate the lives of all around. The most empathetic nurture everyone they meet.

Fromm also gives a scale from narcissism – or complete self-involvement – to love. He believes that love consists of care, responsibility, respect and knowledge.[277] Fromm asserted that love is active, so it is an art, rather than an attraction. He gives the metaphor of a painter who waits until the right scene appears before learning how to paint, believing that the skill will come from the scene. In Fromm's terms, we need to learn how to love – and firstly how to accept and love ourselves – before we can truly experience love.

Fromm's third scale in *The Art of Loving* is from dependence to independence. When we are born, we are completely dependent. To reach maturity means to achieve independence and the ability to make independent decisions as well as emotional autonomy. The truly mature person has love for all of humanity, not simply for a family, tribe or nation, and understands that independence leads to interdependence. The mature person can be depended upon and understands that we all depend upon one another.

We have to be careful that our certainties are based upon the best evidence and direct us in a life-affirming, pro-social way. The simple truth is that *we behave as we believe*, so it is vital that we are willing to question our beliefs. By recognizing and overcoming manipulation or coercive control, we can greatly reduce conflict, better conserve our environment and lead more fulfilling lives. We have the tools to make a better world, and we have the ability to use those tools.

recommended reading:

Ira Chaleff, *Intelligent Disobedience: Doing Right When What You're Told to Do is Wrong*
John Stuart Mill, *On Liberty*
Erich Fromm, *The Art of Loving*

Appendix A

Dr Philip Zimbardo on mind control:
A basic value of the profession of psychology is promoting human freedom of responsible action... and supporting an individual's rights to exercise them. Whatever we mean by 'mind control' stands in opposition to this positive value orientation... mind control is neither magical nor mystical, but a process that involves a set of basic social psychological principles. Conformity, compliance, persuasion, dissonance, reactance, guilt and fear arousal, modelling and identification are some of the staple social influence ingredients well studied in psychological experiments and field studies. In some combinations, they create a powerful crucible of extreme mental and behavioral manipulation when synthesized with several other real-world factors, such as charismatic, authoritarian leaders, dominant ideologies, social isolation, physical debilitation, induced phobias, and extreme threats or promised rewards that are typically deceptively orchestrated, over an extended period in settings where they are applied intensively. A body of social science evidence shows that when systematically practiced by state-sanctioned police, military or destructive cults, mind control can induce false confessions, create converts who willingly torture or kill 'invented enemies,' engage indoctrinated members to work tirelessly, give up their money—and even their lives—for 'the cause'.

Philip Zimbardo, President's Column of the APA Monitor, American Psychology Association. Reproduced with the kind permission of Dr Zimbardo.

Appendix B

Professor Alan Scheflin's Social Influence Model (SIM)

Law Professor Alan W. Scheflin coined the phrase The Myth of the Unmalleable Mind which is the basic belief that we are in control of our own minds and cannot be unfairly influenced outside of our awareness. This is a comforting thought; however, history has shown that this "comforting thought" is a myth. Most readers of this book have come to this understanding the hard way.

Let us suppose you believe that you have been a victim of an impermissible form of mind manipulation or coercive thought control. And you now want to sue the perpetrators. The first problem you will encounter is finding an attorney sufficiently qualified to handle these very specialized types of cases.

While "cultic" organizations and other persuasion groups are armed with attorneys well versed in defending their clients in these cases, there are very few lawyers with expertise in advocating for injured parties such as yourself who have been the victims of such organizations. Once you have found an attorney willing to take your case to court, there are new hurdles to conquer.

In the past, judges have refused to step into litigation that involved topics such as "brainwashing" or "mind control" or "thought reform." What plaintiffs needed was a recognized legal theory that would open the doors to the courtroom. They found such a theory in the concept of "undue influence," which has been recognized for hundreds of years as providing monetary relief for people who have essentially been swindled out of their money.

Fortunately, in recent years legislatures have added new laws making it easier to obtain financial compensation when "coercive control" or "predatory alienation" has been involved.

At this point, the attorney must prove that you, the plaintiff-victim, were taken advantage of in such a manner that justice demands relief. To accomplish this goal, Professor Scheflin created the Social Influence Model (SIM) in 2015.

Professor Scheflin's inspiration came from a section of Rudyard Kipling's poem My Six Servants, published in *JustSo Stories* (1902):

I keep six honest serving-men
They taught me all they knew;
Their names are *What* and *Why* and *When*
And *How* and *Where* and *Who*.

The Social Influence Model (SIM) has these six components:

1. Influencer [Identity and Status] [Who]
2. Influencer's Motives [Purpose] [Why]
3. Influencer's Methods [Techniques] [What/How]
4. Circumstances [Timing & Setting] [Where/When]
5. Influencee's Receptivity/Vulnerability [Individual Differences] [Who]
6. Consequences [Results] [What]

The SIM is designed to be a benefit to five different audiences:

1. Victims - You are going to court because you have been made a victim by the person or organization you are now suing. In order to assist your lawyer, you will need to provide him or her with a factual description of what happened to you over the course of your mental enslavement. Interestingly, the Kipling poem is taught in journalism courses as a guide for reporters to be able to present the most instructive and compelling story. Readers of such stories will have the most complete understanding of what happened when each of the Six Servants is represented.

In bringing a legal case, you are the reporter of your own story, and need to provide to your lawyer each of the Six Servants in order for him or her to present the facts by which the judge and jury can comprehend fully the circumstances that have brought you before them. Your lawyer will want to know what happened to you, when it took place, where it took place, how it happened, why it happened, and who was involved in making it happen. It is always advisable to put your presentation into a chronological format and to state carefully the various details, both factual and emotional, of your experience. This process should help clarify the experience you had and enable both you and others to view it clearly and dispassionately.

2. Lawyers - A good lawyer must make your case come alive in the hearts and minds of the jurors and the judge. Factual evidence and scientific evidence must be woven together to fit into the legal theory your lawyer will present. Every legal theory has certain elements which must be proven before financial compensation can be awarded.

For lawyers, the SIM has several purposes. Lawyers prove their cases by presenting witnesses to explain the facts and experts to explain the science. A lawyer could make a chart of the SIM and include the information you have provided and the testimony witnesses and experts will give. Lawyers long ago discovered that the eye is more powerful than the ear. While jurors can hear evidence, it is much more dramatic if they see a visual representation of it. For example, in a case involving an automobile and locomotive collision, a lawyer in a courtroom brought in a full-sized model of the front of a train engine, which had a much more formidable impact than just referring to the train. In another case involving overcrowding in prisons, a lawyer constructed a life size mock-up of a prison cell so jurors could see how physically confining it was when an excessive number of prisoners were put into it.

Similarly, charts and graphs in which evidence and science has been summarized into categories is more compelling than jurors being asked to remember hours and hours of often technical testimony. The SIM also focuses the lawyer's attention by directing the jurors' attention to each element that must be proven in order for you to prevail. Indeed, most presentations given by lecturers involve some type of PowerPoint or similar computer assisted visual presentations. A further benefit is that the organization of each of the elements aids the jurors in providing a structure for their deliberations.

3. Experts - It is the job of expert witnesses to explain science to the jury and judge. With regard to cases involving allegations of some type of mind control or undue influence, technical scientific data can be more easily structured using the SIM. For example, the Influencer's Methods may involve a variety of psychological persuasion techniques carefully used on innocent victims unaware that they are being manipulated. To take an easy example, in cases involving various aspects of child abuse and seduction, an expert might present evidence of what is called "grooming," with the accompanying scientific literature supporting how what seems to start as an innocent introduction to someone leads to their mental and physical domination.

Another example involves the Influencee's Receptivity/Vulnerability. It is well known that people have different personality styles. Some people are more susceptible to influence than others. This is often called Individual Differences.

There are various scientific testing instruments that can determine a person's receptivity to suggestion or influence. These scales often appear in cases involving hypnosis and cases involving police interrogation. Because expert testimony is often the most difficult for jurors to process, the SIM provides a visual reminder of why jurors are hearing this particular expert testimony and why it is relevant to the resolution of the case.

There are volumes of books and manuals for salespeople and telemarketers where they are taught a variety of techniques for keeping a potential customer engaged until the point of sale. In fact, this is another example of grooming. This knowledge is usually outside the realm of the victim's conscious understanding.

4. Jurors - Jurors appreciate having evidence organized for them. In court, evidence is usually not presented in a sequential manner, especially given the fact that two sides deliver entirely different conceptions of what the case is about and the nature of the relevant facts. The SIM allows the jurors to take both sides of the case and understand how to make decisions of what evidence to accept or reject. It gives them a clearer path to the verdict they will reach. Jurors appreciate that.

5. Judges - For the same reasons that the SIM is persuasive for jurors; it is also persuasive for judges. A judge decides what evidence is admissible, what legal theories are permissible, and what jury instructions are acceptable. Jurors may ultimately decide the case, but it the judge who is the gatekeeper as to what evidence the jury can hear and what expert testimony is relevant. The SIM is a useful structure for the judge to understand the significance of certain expert testimony that the judge might otherwise consider irrelevant. Judges appreciate when a lawyer has made their task easier.

Conclusion: We began with the Myth of the Unmalleable Mind and we conclude with the Myth of Irreversible Mind Control. This is the belief that mind control techniques turn people into human robots who cannot be salvaged. Just as people are wrong to believe their minds cannot be unduly influenced, people are wrong to believe that once having fallen under the influence, people cannot be brought back to their senses. Indeed, the SIM is part of the process of this reverse engineering.

For many people, the greatest threat, often unthought and unspoken, is that other people can comfortably be doing their thinking for them. Group conformity is easier than individual responsibility, but it also diminishes the soul. We should concentrate less on teaching people *what* to think, and more on *how* to think.

The United States Supreme Court in 1969 in Stanley v. Georgia [394 U.S. 557] said: "Our whole constitutional heritage rebels at the thought of giving government the power to control men's minds." Our whole human heritage should rebel at the thought of giving people the power to control men's minds.[278]

Appendix C

Other Specified Dissociative Disorder 300.15 is an "Identity disturbance due to prolonged and intense coercive persuasion: Individuals who have been subjected to intense coercive persuasion (i.e. brainwashing, thought reform, indoctrination while captive, torture, long-term political imprisonment, recruitment by sects/cults or by terror organizations) may present with prolonged changes in, or conscious questioning of, their identity."

Diagnostic and Statistical Manual of Mental Disorders, Fifth Edition (DSM-5), American Psychiatric Association, 2013

afterword: the Open Minds Foundation

The first edition of this book was written in 2015 as the first project of the Open Minds Foundation, a tax-exempt 501 (c) (3) organization based in the US. I worked for five years to establish the foundation, contributing almost 200 pieces to the website, and editing more than 200 others, with the constant help and support of my assistant Spike Robinson.

As Richard Kelly has said, "After Jon introduced me to his older brother Jim, also a businessman, we created a plan to share Jon's unique knowledge with the world." The Open Minds Foundation was the fruit of that plan.

Spike and I withdrew from the foundation to create the YouTube channel Jon Atack, friends and family. Although I am no longer involved with the foundation on a day-to-day basis, I continue to contribute to it, and urge readers to look at the wealth of material available on its website: https://www.openmindsfoundation.org/

acknowledgments

My first thanks are due to my brother Jim and his wife Janet. This book would not have been possible without their unstinting support. Indeed, none of my work these last twenty-five years would have been possible without their unselfish generosity. My brother Andrew has provided help and advice in matters practical these many years, and I also appreciate the constant support of his wife Sarah.

The book was outlined with the help of my dear friend Christian Szurko, who has four decades of experience helping former members of authoritarian groups. Several chapters belong to a more substantial work, written with the encouragement and editorial assistance of Jonny Jacobsen. Professor Khapta Akhmedova kindly reviewed the chapter where her remarkable work is discussed.

Dick Kelly suggested that I distil my thoughts into a short book. He provided editorial suggestions through the various editions.

A number of friends have provided editorial comment, most significantly Alan Scheflin, Spike Robinson, Jessica Terwiel, Mark Laxer and Pamela Davies. Spike has been untiring in her devotion and undone many a grammatical lapse, added several of her own illustrations, and also provided the glowing "about the author" section. Jessica shared her expertise with a complete review of the book.

Yuval Laor's critique has been essential. He has kindly shared his groundbreaking ideas about the evolution of love, of belief and of fervor with me since we met in 2015. Criminologist Julia Gutgsell also provided helpful comments to several chapters.

Steven Hassan has been a constant supporter of my work for many years, for which I am most grateful. I would also like to thank Nick Child,

Gail Benton, Mike Finch, Bonnie Zieman, Mariuca Rofic, Carmen, Louise, Flunk, David H, Eddie Stratton, Dave, Rex Basterfield, Chris Shelton, Tony Ortega, Professor Alexander Dvorkin, Jeffrey Jay and Betsy for their useful and heartening comments. The author's path is always lonely, and I am grateful to everyone who has offered support and encouragement along the way. The book was prepared for publication by Spike Robinson and finalized by Mike White at Ghost River Images.

I am also grateful to Frances Peters, Lee Marsh, Kirk Honda, Rachel Bernstein, Pearse Redmond, Hoyt Richards, Pat Ryan, Joe Kelly, Joe Szimhart, Rod and Linda Dubrow-Marshall, Ken Bernstein, James Beverley, Pete Griffiths, Michelle Haslam, Tilman Hausherr, Karin Spaink, Tony Ortega, David Hensel, Laurent, Bonnie and Richard Woods, Roger Nygard and Jamie de Wolf.

My work has long been inspired by my friends and co-workers, in particular, Ira Chaleff, Steven Hassan, Yuval Laor and, as ever, Christian Szurko. I also have a debt to my late friends and colleagues Louis Jolyon West, Margaret Singer and Betty Tylden. All of the authors mentioned in this book have informed and inspired me, most especially Robert Jay Lifton, Philip Zimbardo, Leon Festinger, Muzafer Sherif, Stanley Milgram, Solomon Asch, Norman Cohn, Eli Sagan, Barbara Tuchman, V.S. Ramachandran, Oliver Sacks, Robert Cialdini, Anthony Pratkanis, Elliot Aronson, Aaron Beck, Alan Scheflin, Stuart Ewan, Naomi Klein, Nancy Snow, Robert A Burton, Merlin Donald, Erich Fromm, David Robson and Janja Lalich.

For their considerable help in improving and sustaining my health over the years, I'd like to thank Ram Patel, John Abercrombie and my friend Rob Mason and his team at Dent Blanche.

My gratitude will always be due to my children Ben, Elisabeth, Sam and Dan, and to my extended family, especially Amelie and Aarti. They are a constant source of inspiration and listen patiently – save for Amelie, who is only eight – and offer their own frequently useful insights. I am particularly grateful to Sam for his observation that sociopaths are not affected by groupthink, and to Dan for his prodigious memory when small details are called for. With the launch of our YouTube channel, Sam has become vital to my exploration of the topics in this book. Without my beloved Pamela nothing would be possible.

about the author

Born in the cathedral city of Lichfield, UK, Jon Atack has always been fascinated with the workings of the human mind. He draws his perspective and streetwise, yet compassionate, wisdom from hundreds of interviews with the survivors of coercive control in a career spanning almost four decades. Widely acclaimed in academic circles not only for his talents as a historian and researcher, but also his sharp wit and social insight, he honed his skills while deconstructing the labyrinthine net of lies surrounding authoritarian group leader Ron Hubbard in the 1980s. Having devoted many years to helping former Scientologists recover their mental equilibrium and spiritual independence, in the early 1990s, he turned his attention to the wider problems of unethical persuasion, not only in abusive groups but in our culture at large. He works to educate the public on the social manipulation we all face in our daily lives. He lives in a quiet village near Nottingham, England, where, following Voltaire's advice, he cultivates his garden, and also his four children and his grandchild Amelie .

~ Spike Robinson

Jon is the author of the only history of Scientology, the best-selling *Let's Sell These People a Piece of Blue Sky*. His introduction to that subject is

Scientology: The Cult of Greed. He has published two novels, *Voodoo Child (slight return)* and *Halcyon Daze* and a translation of Lao Tze's *Tao Te Ching.*

Find out more at Amazon.com/author/jonatack
Check jon atack, family and friends on YouTube
Please post reviews online at book sellers
and on social media!

references

1   Dictionary.com

2   Pratkanis & Shadel, *Weapons of Fraud*, AARP, Seattle, 2005.

3   Robert Cialdini, *Influence: The Psychology of Persuasion*, Harper, NY, 2007

4   The Hill and Knowlton agency and Jack Trout have been on the Scientology payroll.

5   Margaret Thaler Singer with Janja Lalich, *op. cit.* While "cult" groups in western society tend to consist of educated seekers, this is not true of popular movements, from football hooligans and gangs, to the grass roots support for Nazism. In the US, Identity Christians do not fit the profile of other more sophisticated groups, either. Groups such as the Watchtower Society – or Jehovah's Witnesses – restrict education for their members, and actively recruit from prison populations.

6   "the outstanding common characteristic of terrorists is their normality," Martha Crenshaw (1981 study of the Algerian FLN), "terrorists do not show any striking psychopathology," McCauley and Segal (1987) cited by Jerold M. Post, *Leaders and Their Followers in a Dangerous World*, New York, 2004, p.128; see also Marc Sageman, *Understanding Terror Networks*, Philadelphia, 2004; Anne Speckhard & Khapta Ahkmedova, *The Making of a Martyr: Chechen Suicide Terrorism*, Studies in Conflict and Terrorism , Volume 29, Issue 5, pgs. 1-65. 2006. See also Ariel Merari, *Driven to Death* (OUP, 2010), and https://rusi.org/sites/default/files/201602_clat_policy_paper_1_v2.pdf which estimates mental illness at 27% in the normal population and 35% in terrorists

7   *A Course in the Art of Recruiting*, Abu Amru Al Qa'idy

8   Yuval Laor, PhD thesis, *The Religious Ape*.

9   *ibid.* See also Yuval's work on our jon attack, family and friends YouTube channel

10   See, for instance, Mircea Eliade, *A History of Religious Ideas,* volume 1, *From the Stone Age to the Eleusinian Mysteries*, University of Chicago Press, 1978

11   https://en.wikipedia.org/wiki/Mithraism#cite_note-RichardsonHopfe1994-7

12   For an overview of Gnostic Christianity, see Elaine Pagels, *Gnostic Gospels*, Random House, NY, 2004

13   11 March 2001, The Telegraph, *Straw scores own goal with Freemasons' register*

https://www.telegraph.co.uk/news/uknews/1325935/Straw-scores-own-goal-with-Freemasons-register.html

14   *Revealed: How gangs used the Freemasons to corrupt police,* 13 January 2014, The Independent

15   https://www.theguardian.com/uk-news/2018/feb/05/freemasons-in-westminster-should-declare-membership-tory-mp-journalists; https://www.theguardian.com/politics/2018/feb/04/two-freemasons-lodges-operating-secretly-at-westminster

16   Ron Hubbard, *An Open Letter to All Clears*, Policy Letter, 17 January 1967: "your first duty is to protect the repute of the state of Clear by exemplary conduct."

17   Robert Jay Lifton, *Thought Reform and the Psychology of Totalism: A Study of "Brainwashing" in China*, Norton Library, NY, 1963, 1969

18   Robert Jay Lifton, *Destroying the World to Save It*, Henry Holt, NY, 1999

19   https://www.youtube.com/watch?v=F2XkzZvbJCg

20   Ma Anand Sheela, *Don't Kill Him! The story of my life with Bhagwan Rajneesh*, Prakash Books, New Delhi, 2012, 2018.

21   Margaret Thaler Singer with Janja Lalich, *op. cit.*, p.xix.

22   Encyclopaedia Britannica online: "Among the first new religions in the United States were the Seventh-day Adventists and the Jehovah's Witnesses, both the products of millenarian fervour set off in the mid-19th century by William Miller (1782–1849)." Murray Rubenstein. Accessed 26 February 2020.

23   "The pioneer New Religious Movement, Latter Day Saint Movement and The Church of Jesus Christ of Latter-day Saints, date back to 1830." John Misachi, World Atlas online, https://www. worldatlas.com/articles/what-is-a-new-religious-movement.html, accessed 26 February 2020.

24   Eileen Barker, *New Religious Movements*, HMSO, London, 1989, p.9 "most of which have emerged in their present form since the 1950s".

25   Jon Atack, Response to Benjamin Zeller's article: *The Cult of Trump? What "Cult Rhetoric" Actually Reveals*, in Religion & Politics, October 29, 2019

26   Shorter Oxford English Dictionary, vol.1, OUP, 1977.

27   Bryan Wilson, *The Social Dimensions of Sectarianism: Sects and New Religious Movements in Contemporary Society*, Clarendon, Oxford, 1990

28   Robert Jay Lifton, M.D., *Losing Reality: on cults, cultism, and the mindset of political and religious zealotry*, New Press, NY and London, 2019.

29   Definition formulated, in 1985, at a Conference on Cults and Society arranged by the American Family Foundation, chaired by Professor Louis Jolyon West, M.D., cited by Singer & Addis, *Cults, Coercion, and Contumely*, published in eds. Kales, Pearce & Greenblatt, *The Mosaic of Contemporary Psychiatry in Perspective*, Springer-Verlag, NY, 1992. Also cited in West & Martin. See Singer & Lalich, *Cults in Our Midst*, for a thorough definition of "cult" attributes.

30   Margaret Singer and Janja Lalich, *Cults in Our Midst: The Hidden Menace in Our Everyday Lives*, Jossey-Bass, San Francisco, 1995, p.17.

31   Charles Mackay, *Extraordinary Popular Delusions and the Madness of Crowds*, Wordsworth Editions, Ware, Hertforshire, 1995; first edition 1841 and 1852.

32   https://en.wikipedia.org/wiki/Trofim_Lysenko

33   Ben Goldacre, *Bad Science*, Fourth Estate, London, 2008.

34   This chapter is adapted from the author's work-in-progress *Waking Reason*.

35   Janja Lalich, *Bounded Choice: True Believers and Charismatic Cults*, University of California, Berkeley, 2004

36   Merriam Webster, https://www.merriam-webster.com/words-at-play/brainwashing-word-history, accessed 28 January 2020

37   Professor Richard L Walker, *China Under Communism: The First Five Years*, 1955 Yale University Press, New Haven, p.53.,

38   Professor Aminda Smith, *Thought Reform and China's Dangerous Classes: Reeducation, Resistance, and the People*, Rowman & Littlefield, London, 2012.

39   Richard L. Walker, *ibid*, p.54.

40   Richard L. Walker, *ibid*, p.54.

41   In 2018, "re-education" camps were alleged to hold more than one million people. https://www.bbc.co.uk/news/world-asia-china-45147972, accessed 25 October 2018.

42   New York Times, *China Wants the World to Stay Silent on Muslim Camps. It's Succeeding*, 25 September 2019.

43   However, it does seem likely that the US had used cluster units that released insects carrying biological agents. It is worth considering the Chinese sponsored International Report, available at https://www.documentcloud.org/documents/4334133-ISC-Full-Report-Pub-Copy.html

44   see Steve Hassan's *Detailed Information on the Moon Organization, History of Organization*. http://www.freedomofmind.com/resourcecenter/groups/m/moonies/moonhistory.htm

45   Robert Jay Lifton, *Thought Reform and the Psychology of Totalism, op.cit*, 1969, p.420.

46   Steven Hassan, *Releasing the Bonds*, Freedom of Mind Press, Somerville, MA, 2000; also, Hassan, *Combating Cult Mind Control*, second revised edition, 2015.

47   *Mystery of the last hours of failed suicide bomber found dead in sea*, Chris McGreal and Jeevan Vasagar, The Guardian, 20 May 2003.

48   *What turned two happy teenagers into hate-driven suicide bombers?*, Nick Britten, Rosie Waterhouse and Sean O'Neill, Daily Telegraph, filed 2 May 2003.

49   Sharif Maher, *Glasgow bombs: the doctor I knew*, New Statesman, 5 July 2007; BBC News channel, *Bomb plot: Arrests and releases*, 5 October 2007.

50   Zimbardo and Lieppe, *The Psychology of Attitude Change and Social Influence*, McGraw Hill, NY, 1991, p.10.

51   Marc Sageman, *Understanding Terror Networks*, Penn, University of Philadelphia Press, 2004, p.92.

52   Ed Husain, *The Islamist*, Penguin, London, 2007, p.73. I use the term "Islamist" to mean a Muslim who sees the faith as political.

53   Husain, *ibid*, p.3

54   Husain, *ibid*, p.70ff.

55   Husain, *ibid*, pp.108, 113, 116, 117, 153. When Scientology was banned in three Australian states it simply restyled itself "The Church of the New Faith" until the ban was lifted.

56   BBC Panorama, *Faith, Hate and Charity*, 2006.

57   In Great Britain, there are more than 1200 mosques - https://www.mabonline.net/mosques-in-britain/ These are monitored for 'hate speech' – a crime in the UK – by the security services.

58   Husain, *op. cit.*, p.77.

59   Husain, *ibid*, p.38.

60   L. Ron Hubbard, Policy Letter, *Flowers, Care Of*, 9 September 1965.

61   Husain, *op. cit.*, pp.81-82.

62   If Chamberlain had not "appeased" Hitler in Munich in 1938, Britain would almost certainly have lost the war. There were only 12 high altitude fighter aircraft in service in Britain at the time. Under Chamberlain's direction, Britain was out-producing Germany in fighter aircraft by the time the Battle of Brtain began, in July 1940.

63   suras 5:29, 5:32; 18:74; see http://islamicsupremecouncil.org/understanding-islam/legal-rulings/21-jihad-classical-islamic-perspective.html and http://www.meforum.org/5320/islam-suicide-bombings

64   Husain, *op. cit.*, p.52.

65   Lifton, *Thought Reform*, *op. cit..*, p.429.

66   a swastika has been discovered that is 12,000 years old, see Joseph Campbell, *The Flight of the Wild Gander*, Viking Press, NY, 1969.

67   Husain, *op. cit.*, p.71.

68   according to the Hizb, for thirteen centuries, when the last sultan was removed, in 1924, Husain, *ibid*, pp.134-135.

69   *There Can Be No End to Jihad*, Christianity Today, 31 January 2005.

70   Husain, *op. cit.*, p.145.

71   Lifton, *Thought Reform*, p.424.

72   "mystical manipulation" and "planned spontaneity" in Lifton's model.

73   Robert Jay Lifton, *Destroying the World to Save It*, *op. cit*, 1999. The doctrine of *poa* is an ancient Buddhist idea, but separated by Shoko Asahara from the more fundamental doctrine of compassion.

74   Husain, *op. cit.*, p.147.

75   *Captive Minds: Hypnosis and Beyond*, Pierre Lasry, Canada, 1983.

76   Lifton, *Thought Reform*, op. cit., p.432.

77   *ibid*, p.431.

78   Singer and Lalich, *op. cit.*

79   for a more complete explanation of Occam's razor, see http://en.wikipedia.org/wiki/Occam's_razor

80   Lifton, *Thought Reform*, op. cit., p.428.

81   Stephen Kent, *Degrees of Embellishment: Scientology, L. Ron Hubbard, and His Civil Engineering Credentials Fraud*, CESNUR Journal, 2020, DOI: 10.26338/tjoc.2020.supp.3.1

82   Lifton, *Destroying the World to Save It*, *op. cit*, p.67.

83   Husain, *op. cit.*, pp.151-153.

84   *There Can Be No End to Jihad*, *op. cit.*

85   *Attack on London "inevitable"*, The Age, 19 April 2004.

86   this chapter is adapted from the author's work in progress *Waking Reason*.

87   Gustave Le Bon, *The Crowd*, Macmillan, NY, 1896.

88   For the satisfaction of fellow pedants, the possessive apostrophe is not used in the place name "Robbers Cave".

89   Psychologist Gina Perry has criticised the Robbers Cave study, see her interview with participant experimenter O.J. Harvey. There is evidence that the boys were influenced by the experimenters.

See also https://www.theguardian.com/books/2020/may/09/the-real-lord-of-the-flies-what-happened-when-six-boys-were-shipwrecked-for-15-months which shows that without a predator in the group, people can adapt peacefully to a threatening situation.

90   Muzafer Sherif, O. J. Harvey, B. Jack White, William R. Hood, Carolyn W. Sherif, *Intergroup Conflict and Cooperation: The Robbers Cave Experiment*, 1954, study published 1961. http://psychclassics.yorku.ca/Sherif/

91   Andrew Davies, *Gangs of Manchester*, Milo Books, London, 2008.

92   Aaron Beck, *Prisoners of Hate*, HarperCollins, NY, 1999, p.304f.

93   see the Propaganda Model as described by Herman and Chomsky in *Manufacturing Consent: The Political Economy of the Mass Media*, Bodley Head, London, 2008.

94   Economist Thibauld le Texier has critised the Stanford Prison Experiment in his *Histoire d'un Mensonge* ("the history of a lie"), Éditions La Découverte, Paris, 2018. He relies upon Professor Zimbardo's own meticulous recordings and the accounts of former participants – largely made long after the events.

95   Zimbardo, *The Lucifer Effect: How good people turn evil*, Random House, US, 2007, p.30. This is an essential text.

96   *ibid*, pp.32&33.

97   *ibid*, p.59.

98   *ibid*, p.60.

99   In keeping with Christopher Simpson's claims that almost all post-war funding for social science in the US was military (see reference note, chapter 1), the Stanford Prison Experiment was funded by the Office of Naval Research, Zimbardo, *ibid*, p.236. [does this footnote fit?]

100   *ibid*, p.77.

101   *ibid*, p.107.

102   the first "prisoner" to withdraw would later claim that he simply wanted to leave, so made up his reaction. As the students were all told they could leave at any moment, this is difficult to believe. Zimbardo made his recordings freely available and on one a guard is encouraged by an experimenter to act more strongly. This does not invalidate the experiment.

103   Stephen Reicher and S. Alexander Haslam, *Rethinking the psychology of tyranny: The BBC prison study,* British Psychological Society, 2005.

104   Zimbardo, *Lucifer Effect*, p.20.

105   Stanley Milgram, *Obedience to Authority*, NY, Harper & Row, 1974, p.23.

106   see http://www.videosift.com/video/The-Original-Milgram-Experiment-1961; Some researchers believe the participants in the experiment – and in all the replications of the experiment – knew the "student" was acting, see K.M. Taylor and J.A. Shepperd, *Probing Suspicion Among Participants in Deception Research*, American Psychologist 51, no.8 (1996), pp.886-887, cited by Aaron Beck, *Prisoners of Hate*, p.309. However, in 1972, Sheridan and King published a study showing that

20 out of 26 participants gave real shocks to a puppy that was "running, howling and yelping". Milgram had this to say, "At many points we attempted to establish a boundary. Cries from the victims were inserted: they were not effective enough. The victim claimed heart trouble; subjects still shocked him on command. The victim pleaded that he be let free and his answers no longer registered on the signal box: subjects continued to shock him." Milgram, *op. cit.,* p.188. Milgram's remarkable book shows that he checked many permutations of the experiment.

107   Milgram, *op. cit.,* p.188.

108   Festinger, Riecken, Schacter, *op. cit.*, p.56.

109   *ibid.*

110   "changed date: failed predictions", *JWFacts* http://www.jwfacts.com/watchtower/1800s.php

111   for a full discussion of cognitive dissonance, see Harmon-Jones & Mills, eds, *Cognitive dissonance: progress on a pivotal theory in social psychology*, American Psychological Association, Washington, DC, 1999.

112   Harmon-Jones & Mills, *op. cit.*, pp.3-10.

113   see *Asch S. E. (1956) Studies of independence and conformity* at http://www.gerardkeegan.co.uk/resource/seminalstudies.htm

114   Replication with different groups has produced varying results. In one experiment, science students showed virtually no compliance, *ibid.* Keegan references Perrin and Spencer, 1980, 1981; Nicholson, N., Cole, S. & Rocklin, T, 1985; Lalancette, M-F & Standing, L.G, 1990;Neto, F. 1995.

115   Gina Kolta, *Study Finds Big Social Factor in Quitting Smoking*, New York Times, 22 May 2008.

116   Khapta Akhmedova, emails to the author, November & December 2008; see also *Mass hysteria: Terror's hidden ally*, New Scientist, 14 October 2006; *Poison in the air*, The Guardian, 1 March 2006; see also *Ethnic strife triggers psychosomatic illness*, New Scientist, 25 January 1997. Two papers are available on this subject, but neither has yet been translated from the Russian: Akhmedova, Khapta (2006), *Factors and Conditions of Mass Sociogenic Illness (the Chechen Case).* J Social and Clinical Psychiatry, Volume 4, 2006; and Akhmedova, Khapta, *Clinical Description of the Seizures of Patients Involved to Mass Sociogenic Illness*, Materials of Russian Psychiatric Conference on Modern Principles of Therapy and Rehabilitation of Patients with Mental Disorders, 2006. I am deeply indebted to Khapta Akhmedova for her painstaking help with this chapter. Any errors are mine.

117   For a detailed account of mass hysteria, see Aldous Huxley, *The Devils of Loudon,* which was the basis for Ken Russell's stylish film, *The Devils.* Arthur Miller's play, *The Crucible*, deals with the Salem witch trials and is also available in two film versions.

118   Bartholomew and Wessely, *Protean nature of mass sociogenic illness: From possessed nuns to chemical and biological terrorism fears*, British Journal of Psychiatry, 2002, 180:300-306. http://bjp.rcpsych.org/cgi/content/full/180/4/300

119   According to William Safire, *New York Times,* 8 August 2004, William H. Whyte coined the term in *Fortune*, March 1952, defining it thus: "Groupthink is becoming a national philosophy ... Groupthink being a coinage – and, admittedly, a loaded one – a working definition is in order. We are not talking about mere instinctive conformity – it is, after all, a perennial failing of mankind.

What we are talking about is a rationalized conformity – an open, articulate philosophy which holds that group values are not only expedient but right and good as well."; see also Irving Janis, *Victims of Groupthink*, Boston, 1972, p. 9 and Janis and Mann, *Decision Making: A Psychological Analysis of Conflict, Choice and Commitment*, Free Press, NY, 1977.

120   quoted in Daniel Goleman, *Vital Lies, Simple Truthes*, Touchstone, NY, 1986, p.181, see also pp.184-189. "...it is hard to believe in retrospect that the president and his advisers felt the plans for a large-scale, complicated military operation that had been on-going for more than a year could be reworked in four days and still offer a high likelihood of success. It is equally amazing that we in the agency agreed so readily." Richard Bissell, CIA Director of Plans, *Memoirs of a Cold Warrior: from Yalta to Bay of Pigs*. Arthur Schlesinger, in the Pulitzer Prize-winning book, *A Thousand Days*: "Fulbright, speaking in an emphatic and incredulous way, denounced the whole idea. The operation, he said, was wildly out of proportion to the threat. It would compromise our moral position in the world and make it impossible for us to protest treaty violations by the Communists. He gave a brave, old-fashioned American speech, honourable, sensible and strong; and he left everyone in the room, except me and perhaps the President, wholly unmoved."

121   Loren Coleman, *The Copycat Effect*, Paraview, NY, 2004. Cho Seung-Hui, who murdered 32 people at Virginia Tech before turning his gun on himself, called the Columbine killers "martyrs". See also Michael Bond, *Can media coverage of suicides inspire copycats?*, 9 May 2007, New Scientist; Laura Spinney, *Why we do what we do*, 31 July 2004, New Scientist; see also Zimbardo and Lieppe, *The Psychology of Attitude Change and Social Influence*, McGraw Hill, NY, 1991, pp.50-51, reporting Albert Bandura"s studies of copycat aggression among children.

122   Sageman, *op. cit.*, p.92.

123   Kurt Lewin's model of coercive persuasion consists of unfreezing, changing and refreezing the identity.

124   Robert Jay Lifton, *Thought Reform and the Psychology of Totalism, op.cit*, 1969, p.420.

125   Rod Bond and Peter B. Smith, University of Sussex, *Culture and Conformity: A Meta-Analysis of Studies Using Asch's (1952b, 1956) Line Judgment Task*, Psychological Bulletin 1996, Vol. 119, No. 1,111-137, American Psychological Association.

126   see the Propaganda Model as described by Herman and Chomsky in *Manufacturing Consent: The Political Economy of the Mass Media*, Bodley Head, London, 2008.

127   Darley, J. M., and Batson, C.D., *From Jerusalem to Jericho: A Study of Situational and Dispositional Variables in Helping Behavior*, Journal of Personality and Social Psychology, 1973, 27, 100-108.

128   Stanley Milgram, *The Perils of Obedience*, Harper's Magazine, 1974, reprinted as *An Experiment in Autonomy* in *The Moral Life*, ed. Louis J Pojman, OUP, NY & Oxford, 2004.

129   Lifton, *Thought Reform*, p.429.

130   George Orwell, *Nineteen Eighty-Four*, Secker & Warburg, London, 1949.

131   Lifton, *Thought Reform, op. cit.*, pp.429-430.

132   Lifton, *Thought Reform, op. cit.*, p.424.

133   H. G. Wells, *In the Country of the Blind*, Complete Short Stories, Benn, London, 1966.

134   Lifton, *Thought Reform, op. cit.,* p.423. Erich Fromm explored this theme as the "pseudo-self" in his 1941 book *Escape from Freedom.*

135   Zimbardo, *op. cit.,* p.187.

136   Robert Jay Lifton, *The Nazi Doctors: Medical Killing and the Psychology of Genocide,* Basic Books, US, 1986.

137   *Jig-Saw Puzzle,* Beggars Banquet, Rolling Stones, 1968.

138   Festinger, Riecken, Schacter, *op. cit.,* p.4.

139   This if the profession of Orwell's hero in *Nineteen Eighty-Four.* Outcasts are dropped down the "memory hole".

140   "The ability of good music to enthral the masses has been sacrificed on the altar of petit-bourgeois formalism," according to a 1936 article in *Pravda* allegedly written at Stalin's behest.

141   Lifton, *Thought Reform, op. cit.,* pp.427-428.

142   Bacon continued, "And though it may meet a greater number and weight of contrary instances, it will, with great and harmful prejudice, ignore or condemn or exclude them by introducing some distinction, in order that the authority of those earlier assumptions may remain intact and unharmed ... The same reasoning can be seen in every superstition, whether in astrology, dreams, omens, nemesis and the like, in which men find such vanities pleasing, and take note of events where they are fulfilled, but where they are not (even if this happens much more often), they disregard them and pass them by. But this evil lurks far more insidiously in philosophies and sciences, in which an opinion once adopted infects and brings under control all the rest ... the human understanding still has this peculiar and perpetual fault of being more moved and excited by affirmatives than by negatives, whereas rightly and properly it ought to give equal weight to both; rather, in fact, in every truly constituted axiom, a negative instance has the greater weight." Francis Bacon, *Novum Organum,* 1620. This is the same Lord Bacon who ruled on Mrs Death's case. [this comes later in the book]

143   Thomas Kuhn's theory of paradigm shift was proposed in 1962, in *The Structure of Scientific Revolutions,* Chicago University Press, 3rd edition, 1996.

144   Hans Franck: TV documentary *War of the World,* part 3; "Frankly, you and I have diametrically different views of the Chinese. You may be dealing with them as human beings, but I regard them as swine. We can do anything with such creatures." Lt Col Ryukichi Tenuka, *ibid;* Blamey, *ibid,* part 4.

145   Philip Zimbardo, *The Lucifer Effect, op.cit.,* p.337.

146   Konrad Lorenz: "[I]t must be the duty of racial hygiene to be attentive to a more severe elimination of morally inferior human beings than is the case today ... otherwise, humanity will ... be annihilated by the degenerative phenomena that accompany domestication." 1940, cited by Lifton, *The Nazi Doctors, op. cit.,* p.134.

147   Baumslag and Pellegrino, *Murderous Medicine,* Greenwood, 2005, p.123. Only 20% of teachers joined the Nazi Party, *ibid.*

148   For an exhaustive examination see Robert Jay Lifton, *The Nazi Doctors op. cit.* Hitler had earlier congratulated the US on its enforced sterilization of tens of thousands of mentally ill people. That

programme was supported, and even applauded, by leaders of the Protestant, Catholic and Jewish communities in America. See Christine Rosen, *Preaching Eugenics*, Oxford, OUP, 2004. See also Stefan Kühl, *The Nazi Connection: Eugenics, American Racism and German National Socialism*, Oxford, OUP, 1994: "The leaders in the German sterilization movement state repeatedly that their legislation was formulated only after careful study of the California experiment ... It would have been impossible, they say, to undertake such a venture involving some 1 million people without drawing heavily upon previous experience elsewhere." p.42. See also http://downsyndromeuprising. blogspot.co.uk/2013/07/a-brief-history-of-down-syndrome-part-6.html which outlines "eugenics" programmes in France, Belgium, Sweden and Great Britain.

149   Robert Jay Lifton, *Thought Reform and the Psychology of Totalism, op.cit,* 1969, p.420.

150   see Robert Jay Lifton, *Destroying the World to Save It, op. cit,* 1999, p.326ff.

151   Adam Curtis's BBC TV documentary series, *The Power of Nightmares,* explores the origins of Al-Qaeda – and its opposition – in some depth. See also Peter Taylor's BBC TV documentaries, *Age of Terror* and Marc Sageman's *Understanding Terror Networks, op. cit.*

152   David Cohen, *All the world's a net,* 13 April 2002, New Scientist.

153   Janja Lalich explores Max Weber's notion of charisma in *Bounded Choice.*

154   Several groups labelled "terrorists" have achieved respectability in government. Former members of the IRA now sit in the Northern Ireland Assembly. Irgun settled into the political scene after the declaration of the State of Israel. Former Mau Mau established the first independent government of Kenya.

155   https://www.youtube.com/playlist?list=PLOprfY0DnRsYv-GuObWtB8kG6JbXy-tNx

156   Leah Remini with Rebecca Paley, *Troublemaker: Surviving Hollywood and Scientology*, Ballantine Books, NY, 2015

157   This chapter is adapted from the author's work-in-progress *Waking Reason.*

158   Jill Bolte Taylor, *My Stroke of Insight: A Brain Scientist's Personal Journey,* 2006, p.19.

159   Opnions are divided on the validity of the Meyers-Briggs test, but the significant difference in responses is worthy of mention. See for instance, https://journals.sagepub.com/doi/abs/10.3102/00346543063004467

160   Flavil Yeakley, ed, *The Discipling Dilemma*, 1988: http://www.somis.org/TDD-01.html p.27.

161   *ibid;* Yeakley became president of the Association for Psychological Type in 1987.

162   Professor Rod Dubrow-Marshall, *The Influence Continuum – the Good, the Dubious, and the Harmful – Evidence and Implications for Policy and Practice in the 21ˢᵗ Century*, International Journal of Cultic Studies. vol.1, no.1, 2010.

163   for instance, Martha Stout in *The Myth of Sanity*

164   Cited in Merlin Donald, *A Mind So Rare*, W.W. Norton, NY and London, 2001

165   *Once Upon a Time*, Laura Spinney, New Scientist, 10 January 2015.

166   Merlin Donald, *A Mind So Rare, op.cit.*

167   *ibid*

168   Brian Eno with Robert Fripp, *Nervenet*, 1992, Warner.

169   A.R. Luria, *The Man With a Shattered World*, 1975, Penguin, Middlesex.

170   In *A Skeptic's Guide to the Mind*, neurologist Robert A Burton suggests that any estimation of the number of neurons in the brain is a guess, and that glial cells (non-neuronal cells which do not produce electrical impulses) may also be significant.

171   Gerald Edelman, *Second Nature: brain science and human knowledge*, Yale University Press, New Haven and London, 2006; Kathleen Taylor, *Brainwashing: The science of thought control*, Oxford University Press, 2004.

172   Gerald Edelman, *op. cit.*

173   The full passage reads, "Man is not capable of thought in any high degree, and even the most spiritual and cultivated of men habitually sees the world and himself through the lenses of delusive formulas and artless simplifications. For it appears to be an inborn and imperative need of all men to regard the self as a unit. However often and however grievously this illusion is shattered, it always mends again. The judge who sits over the murderer and looks into his face, and at one moment recognizes all the emotions and potentialities of the murderer in his own soul and hears the murderer's voice as his own is at the next moment one and indivisible as the judge, and scuttles back into the shell of his cultivated self and does his duty and condemns the murderer to death. And if ever the suspicion of their manifold being dawns upon men of unusual powers and of unusually delicate perceptions, so that, as all genius must, they break through the illusion of the unity of the personality and perceive that the self is made up of a bundle of selves, they have only to say so and at once the majority puts them under lock and key, calls science to aid, establishes schizophrenia and protects humanity from the necessity of hearing the cry of truth from the lips of these unfortunate persons … In reality, however, every ego, so far from being a unity is in the highest degree a manifold world, a constellated heaven, a chaos of forms, of states and stages, of inheritances and potentialities. It appears to be a necessity as imperative as eating and breathing for everyone to be forced to regard this chaos as a unity and to speak of his ego as though it were one-fold and clearly detached and fixed phenomenon. The delusion rests simply upon a false analogy. As a body everyone is single, as a soul never." Herman Hesse, trans Creighton, rev. Sorrell, *Steppenwolf*, 1927, 2001, Penguin Classics, pp.70-72.

174   Alan Watts, with Al Chung-Liang Huang, *Tao: The Watercourse Way*, Arkana, NY, 1975.

175   John Gottman, *The Relationship Cure*, Three Rivers Press, New York, 2001.

176   The term "pseudo-identity" was used by Louise Jolyon West and Paul Martin in "Pseudo-Identity and the Treatment of Personality Change in Victims of Captivity and Cults", in Lynn and Rhue, *Dissociation: Clinical and Theoretical Perspectives*, Guilford Press, NY and London, 1994.

177   See, for instance, Ronnie Janoff-Bulman on denial in *Shattered Assumptions: Towards a New Psychology of Trauma*, Macmillan, NY, 1992

178   E.g., https://www.britannica.com/topic/institutionalization

179   E.g., https://www.scribd.com/document/179357099/Milton-Erickson-THE-CONFUSION-TECHNIQUE-pdf

180   E.g., https://www.thoughtco.com/limbic-system-anatomy-373200

181 Robert Jay Lifton, *The Nazi Doctors: Medical Killing and the Psychology of Genocide*, Basic Books, NY, 2017

182 Chabris and Simons, see http://www.theinvisiblegorilla.com/

183 Inattentional blindness may simply be due to a limit upon processing in the brain and the need to perceive only relevant information. See https://www.newscientist.com/article/mg22129610-600-invisible-what-your-brain-refuses-to-see/

184 https://www.youtube.com/watch?v=idtbswz_mXw

185 *13 More Things: The Nocebo Effect*, New Scientist, 2 September 2009. It seems important to conclude that if there is evidence for cognition in the brain and evidence that physiology can be influenced by thought, the "hard problem" of consciousness itself, which bedevils psychology and philosophy is far from being solved.

186 "hypnagogic reverie" when waking from sleep, and "hypnopompic reverie" when falling asleep.

187 Accounts from countries dominated by the USSR differed over many years from those in western countries.

188 Carl Sagan, *The Demon-Haunted World*, Random House, NY, 1996. Peter Huston, *Night Terrors, Sleep Paralysis, and Devil Stricken Telephone Cords from Hell*, Sceptical Inquirer, Fall 1992. The Nazis did actually build circular machines like the flying saucer a few years before this error of description.

189 See Brown, Scheflin & Hammond, *Memory, Trauma, Treatment and the Law* for an extensive discussion of recovered memory. W.W. Norton and co, NY and London, 1998

190 Ofshe and Watters, *making Monsters: False Memories, Psychotherapy, and Sexual Hysteria*, University of California Press, 1994; Lawrence Wright, *Remembering Satan: a Tragic Case of Recovered Memory*, Vintage, 1995.

191 Brian Inglis, *Trance*, 1989, Grafton Books, London. See Brown, Scheflin & Hammond, *Memory, Trauma, Treatment and the Law* for an extensive discussion of recovered memory. W.W. Norton and co, NY and London, 1998

192 John F Kihlstrom in Nash and Barnier, *The Oxford Handbook of Hypnosis: Theory, Research and Practice*, Oxford Library of Psychology, OUP, 2012. Yuval Laor comments, "this is a problematic definition because it uses the term "hypnotist" as part of defining hypnosis. But as such it is a good definition, because hypnosis depends on what you think it is. Note that the same game with a different title for the hypnotist, is not hypnosis."

193 Derren Brown, *The Heist, 2006;* and *The Assassin* in *The Experiments*, 2011. Derren Brown has also deftly shown that compliance can be achieved *without* trance induction in his remarkable *Pushed to the Edge* (also known as *The Push*) in 2016.

194 Again, Derren Brown has clearly demonstrated this in his show *Messiah, 2005.*

195 http://wcclf.org/wp-content/themes/wccl/pdf/science-and-buddhism.pdf. Some still question this demonstration.

196 Nash and Barnier, eds, *The Oxford Handbook of Hypnosis: Theory Research and Practice*, OUP, 2008

197 https://www.newscientist.com/article/2151137-your-autopilot-mode-is-real-now-we-know-how-the-brain-does-it/

198   Dr Miguel Farias in *The Buddha Pill: Can Meditation Change You?*, pp.158-9, 2nd edition, 2019, Watkins Media Limited, London

199   Nash and Barnier, *op.cit.*

200   Professor Howard Schacter's *How the Mind Forgets and Remembers* is an excellent text, Houghton Mifflin, Boston, 2001.

201   see Aaron Beck, *Prisoners of Hate, op.cit.*

202   Randy Newman says this well – as ever – in *A Few Words in Defense of Our Country.*

203   Pope Saint Pius X was also a drinker of Mariani wine, https://en.wikipedia.org/wiki/Vin_Mariani.

204   http://thenonist.com/index.php/thenonist/permalink/vin_mariani/

205   Erich Fromm, *Escape From Freedom*, Ishi Press, New York and Tokyo, 2011, first edition 1941.

206   Erich Fromm, *The Heart of Man: Its Genius for Good and Evil*, Harper and Row, New York, 1964.

207   See Henry Kamen, *The Spanish Inquisition: A Historical Revision, Fourth Edition*, Yale University Press, 2014

208   Bernays stopped working for tobacco companies once the dangers of smoking had been proven. He also lobbied against the use of tobacco. Edward Bernays, *Propaganda*, Ig publishing, New York, 2005, p.25 (first edition 1928).

209   Stuart Ewen, *PR! A Social History of Spin*, Basic Books, NY, 1996.

210   Opton and Scheflin, *The Mind Manipulators*, Paddington Press, London, 1978; Walter Bowart, *Operation Mind Control*, Fontana, 1978.

211   Naomi Klein, *The Shock Doctrine*, 2008, Penguin, London.

212   The Louise Ogborn story is largely taken from *A hoax most cruel: Caller coaxed McDonald's managers*, Andrew Wolfson, *Louisvilled Courier-Journal*, October 9, 2005.

http://www.courier-journal.com/story/news/local/2005/10/09/a-hoax-most-cruel-caller-coaxed-mcdonalds-managers-/28936597/; see also Ira Chaleff, *Intelligent Disobedience* and https://en.wikipedia.org/wiki/Strip_search_phone_call_scam.

213   https://www.youtube.com/watch?v=UFXeXK3szOk

214   Bertrand Russell, *The Impact of Science on Society*, 1953.

215   Alan W Scheflin, *Supporting Human Rights*, International Cultic Studies Journal, vol.6, 2015.

216   cited by Abraham Nievod, PhD, JD, in *Undue Influence in Contract and Probate Law*. First passage from Francis Bacon, second from Dawson, John P, *Economic Duress—An Essay in Perspective*, Michigan Law Review 253. http://www.csj.org/pub_csj/csj_vol10_no1_93/undue_influence.htm

217   Frederick Taylor, *Exorcising Hitler: The Occupation and Denazification of Germany*, Bloomsbury, London, 2012, p.282.

218   Nievod, *op.cit.*

219   On the notion of free will, see for example, Halligan & Oakley, *Consciousness isn't all about you, you know*, New Scientist, 15 August 2015, no.3034.

220   Scheflin, A. W., & Opton, E. M., Jr., *The Mind Manipulators,* 1978, New York, NY: Paddington Press.

221 Scheflin, A. W., "Supporting Human Rights by Testifying Against Human Wrongs" Paul Martin Lecture, 2014. http://www.icsahome.com/articles/supporting-human-rights

222 *ibid*

223 Derren Brown, *Fear and Faith,* 2012.

224 Derren Brown, *The Heist, op. cit.*

225 Derren Brown, *The Assassin, op. cit.* See also *Messiah, op. cit*, where he convinced leading psychics of his own psychic ability.

226 at least in Brecht's version, *Leben des Galilei.*

227 Concentration camps were previously established by the US in Cuba, in 1896 and in South Africa by the British in 1900.

228 Hubbard, *Education and Dianetics*, 11 November 1950, *Research and Discovery*, volume 4, p.324; see also *Research and Discovery*, volume 3, pp. 246 & 248. In both cases, these are the first editions, quickly withdrawn and replaced with censored versions.

229 https://en.wikipedia.org/wiki/Movement_for_the_Restoration_of_the_Ten_Commandments_of_God

230 I have been unable to find an account of the denazification program beyond a contemporary newspaper account and a few comments in a history of Wilton Park, where hundreds of Nazis were successfully persuaded to renounce their former beliefs. It would be helpful to know how the debates were managed.

231 Sageman, *op.cit*

232 Professor Christopher Simpson, *Science of Coercion, Communication Research & Psychological Warfare 1945-1960*, 1994, OUP, NY: pp.3-4.

233 Festinger, Riecken, Schacter, *When Prophecy Fails,* 1956, University of Minnesota Press.

234 Both the Trump election and Brexit were supported by organizations linked to Trump's largest financial contributor Robert Leroy Mercer – Cambridge Analytica and Aggregate IQ.

235 see my *Scientology: The Church of Hate* for a detailed account of Scientology's attitude towards "apostates".

236 This author believes that Bobby Beausoleil, who committed the first murder, of Gary Hinman, should long ago have been paroled because of Manson's profound influence over him.

237 Evan Stark, *Coercive Control: How Men Entrap Women in Personal Life,* OUP, 2007.

238 I am concerned about the torture of animals in experimental settings. Seligman went on to write about happiness, and has received an enormous grant to research Mindfulness, which this author considers an abuse of valid meditation techniques.

239 https://jackhiggins1995.wordpress.com/2015/08/22/peter-mcbride-a-true-story-of-domestic-violence-towards-men/

240   L. Laming, *The Victoria Climbié Inquiry. Paper presented to Parliament by the Secretary of State for Health and the Secretary of State for the Home Department*, Crown Copyright, 2003, cited in Patricia McKinsey Crittenden, *Raising Parents: Attachment, representation, and treatment*, Routledge, London and NY, second edition, 2016.

241   Dan Jones interview with Terrie Moffitt, *What Makes a Criminal?*, New Scientist 3290, 11 July 2020.

242   *Frat Boys*, BBC This Week, 2016.

243   http://www.dailymail.co.uk/femail/article-3654776/College-student-recalls-brutally-beaten-boat-paddles-urinated-branded-horrific-hazing-ritual-new-documentary-exposing-dark-fraternities.html

244   https://www.hop-law.com/family-settles-lawsuit-relating-to-hazing-death-of-fraternity-pledge/

245   https://hazingprevention.org/

246   BBC News, 22 July 2016: http://www.bbc.co.uk/news/uk-england-derbyshire-36855374

247   Samuel Clemens (Mark Twain), *Christian Science*, 1907, reprinted by Starling and Black, 2013, p.61.

248   Dan Jones interview with Terrie Moffitt, *op.cit.*

249   Robert Hare, *Without Conscience: The Disturbing World of the Psychopaths Among Us*, Pocket Books, NY, 1995. See also, Hare and Babiak, *Snakes in Suits: When Psychopaths Go to Work*, HarperCollins, NY, 2006.

250   Hare and Babiak, *op.cit*

251   Erich Fromm, *The Heart of Man, op.cit.*

252   Craig Malkin, *Rethinking Narcissism: The Secret to Recognizing and Coping with Narcissists*, HarperCollins, NY, 2015.

253   Jane and Tim McGregor, *The Empathy Trap: Understanding Antisocial Personalities*, Sheldon Press, London, 2013

254   Emma Young, *All About Me*, New Scientist, 9 July 2016; Carol Clark, *Grandiose narcissism reflects U.S. presidents" bright and dark sides*, eScience Commons, Emory University, 5 November 2013.

255   Erich Fromm, *The Heart of Man, op.cit.*

256   Dan Shaw, *Traumatic Narcissism: relational systems of subjugation*, Routledge, NY & London, 2014.

257   A notable exception seems to be the Indus Valley civilization which thrived from 2600-1900 BCE. This proves that it is possible to have a civilization without dictators – or warfare.

258   David Robson, *The Intelligence Trap: Why smart people do stupid things and how to make wiser decisions*, Hodder and Stoughton, London, 2019

259   Emma Young, Evolution tells us why there are two types of leader in today's world, New Scientist, 1 July 2020.

260   Emma Young, *How sharing other people's feelings can make you sick*, New Scientist, 11 May 2016; http://www.compassion-training.org/?lang=en&page=home

261   Paul Bloom, *Against Empathy: The Case for Rational Compassion*, Bodley Head, London, 2016.

262   Carol Clark, *op cit*

263   Craig Malkin, Rethinking Narcissism: The Secret to Recognizing and Coping with Narcissists, Harper, NY, 2015.

264   Simon Baron-Cohen, *Zero Degrees of Empathy: a New Theory of Human Cruelty and Kindness*, Penguin, London, 2012.

265   Judith Rich Harris, *The Nurture Assumption: why children turn out the way they do*, Bloomsbury, London, 1998. Professor Steven Pinker called this book "A turning point in the history of psychology." See also Harris's *No Two Alike,* Norton, NY, 2006.

266   http://www.nytimes.com/2008/02/29/world/asia/29iht-profile.1.10568433. html?pagewanted=all&_r=0

267   General Stanley McChrystal, former commander-in-chief in both Iraq and Afghanistan, repudiated the usefulness of torture in a BBC interview in 2018. The movie The Report gives a chilling account of the torture and shows that it was completely ineffective. It also reveals that President Obama vetoed publication of the torture report, which was ultimately published by Senator Dianne Feinstein. See https://www.latimes.com/opinion/op-ed/la-oe-feinstein-torture-report-20141209-story. html

268   Dr Nicki Crowley, Perspectives from front-line exit-workers and exit-counselors on what helps individuals leave cults and radical extremist groups:

A thematic analysis, Salford University, February 2020

269   "bringing the living back to life" is borrowed from the brilliant poet Charles Causley. It is the charge brought against Jesus in *The Ballad of the Bread Man*.

270   James Austin, *Zen Brain Reflections*, MIT Press, Boston, 2010.

271   For a critique of meditation, see Farias and Wikholm, *The Buddha Pill: can meditation change you?*, Watkins, 2015 and Robert Purser, *McMindfulness: How Mindfulness Became the New Capitalist Spirituality*, Repeater Books, London, 2019.

272   As Dr Philip Zimbardo argues persuasively in *The Lucifer Effect, op.cit.*

273   Alan Watts, compiled by Mark Watts, *Still the Mind: an introduction to meditation*, New World Library, San Francisco, 2002

274   These reflections on education were inspired in part by Matthew Lipmann's *Thinking in Education*, Cambridge University Press, 2003. See in particular pp.18-19.

275   https://www.wpr.org/mendota-juvenile-treatment-center-shows-progress-treating-child-psychopaths

276   Erich Fromm, *The Art of Loving*, Harper and Row, NY, 1956.

277   Erich Fromm, *Man for Himself: An enquiry into the psychology of ethics*, Routlegde and Kegan Paul, UK, 1947.

278   See Scheflin, "Supporting Human Rights by Testifying Against Human Wrongs", *International Journal of Cultic Studies*, Vol. 6, 2015, 69-82.

Printed in Great Britain
by Amazon